Leadership to the Limits

Leadership to the Limits

Freedom and Responsibility

Peter Shaw

CANTERBURY
PRESS
Norwich

© Peter Shaw 2020

Published in 2020 by Canterbury Press
Editorial office
3rd Floor, Invicta House,
108–114 Golden Lane,
London EC1Y 0TG, UK
www.canterburypress.co.uk

Canterbury Press is an imprint of Hymns Ancient & Modern Ltd
(a registered charity)

Hymns Ancient & Modern® is a registered trademark of Hymns Ancient &
Modern Ltd
13A Hellesdon Park Road, Norwich,
Norfolk NR6 5DR, UK

British Library Cataloguing in Publication data

A catalogue record for this book is available
from the British Library

978 1-78622-174-2

Printed and bound by
CPI Group (UK) Ltd

With grateful thanks to Tracy Easthope and Jackie Tookey who provide superb practical support and are always cheerful and positive in their approach.

Contents

Section D: Balancing Freedom and Responsibility 85

Section E: Next Steps 109

Foreword

It has been a privilege to be the first job-share partnership to hold a Director General role in the UK Government. We have a joint responsibility for an important area of Government policy where there are major decisions to be taken and policies to be implemented. We are acutely conscious of the responsibilities we carry and the effect on citizens if decisions and actions are less than optimal.

Working as a job-share means we have to be extra clear on the nature of our shared responsibilities and how we will achieve our objectives together. We need to be consistent in using our freedoms to good effect. We need to contract clearly and openly with each other and those we work with so we bring the best out of each other and provide leadership that enables others to make the most of their freedoms and responsibilities.

Good leadership in any sphere requires using freedoms and discretions well. However constrained you feel, there are always choices to be made about the priorities you focus on, the tone you set, and the way you affirm and motivate those around you. There is always more freedom than you might initially think exists. There are always ways in which you can carve out a degree of freedom in the approach you deploy.

Our job-share has given us the freedom to work part-time in challenging and interesting roles, while allowing us to meet our responsibilities to our families as well as at work. We have had to give each other the freedom to operate, with each taking responsibility for delivering for the other as well for ourselves.

Over time our contracting with one another has become second nature, but the ideas in this book have given us an opportunity to pause and re-evaluate.

In this book, Peter draws cogently from his experience as a Director General in the UK Government and his coaching of senior leaders and teams. He sets out a thought-provoking and interesting set of insights, prompting leaders to embrace freedom and to balance it with responsibility in a way that means they are positive about what they are able to move forward and not overwhelmed by competing expectations and pressures.

Ruth Hannant and Polly Payne
Directors General, Rail Group, Department for Transport
London

Introduction

Balancing freedom and responsibility is at the heart of leading well. True freedom means choosing a course of action for which we then take responsibility. Responsibility is only fully owned when it is freely embraced. Self-awareness involves recognizing how we and others respond to responsibility. Stretching our understanding of ourselves and the situations we are in enables us to use our freedoms and our capacity to take on responsibility to new levels. Good leadership involves both pushing boundaries, so that we use our freedoms boldly, and living responsibly so that we do not overwhelm ourselves or those around us.

My encouragement to leaders in any sector or seniority is to reflect regularly on the freedoms they have and how best to exercise them with deliberate intent. It is the freedom to focus on what and who matters to you, alongside a focus on your own wellbeing. Perhaps we can push the limits while recognizing our own limits at the same time.

We all have leadership opportunities in the way we influence others. Using our freedoms to recognize and apply our responsibilities wisely is a privilege and can be a joy. This book is about how we push our boundaries and how we deploy our freedom within a clear understanding of our responsibilities. My intent in this book is to help you recognize what can limit your taking hold of the freedoms you have, and then to enable you to explore your scope to embrace and hold lightly to responsibilities.

We believe that freedom of thought and expression is the hallmark of a civilized society. At the same time, we are horrified by the abuse of freedom by many individuals and groups through emotive social media comments and campaigns that are evidence-light. We are increasingly concerned about extreme newspaper headlines that can stifle constructive, forward-looking debate. We are conscious that hate campaigns are easily fuelled with a growing risk of violence.

The responsible use of freedom is central to a thriving democratic society and any vibrant organization. A healthy organization encourages the freedom to develop initiatives and express opinions. How do we best use that freedom responsibly and not be overwhelmed by it?

We can feel responsible for everything going on around us. How do we handle an overdeveloped sense of responsibility and become liberated from the burdens and responsibilities that can ensnare us? How can we become freer to express our views, develop our contribution and be the most influential person we can be in a way that embraces appropriate responsibility for our actions?

We see many examples of people failing to take responsibility for their actions, such as leaders of organizations or movements resigning immediately after not getting their preferred outcomes and thereby not fulfilling their responsibilities to ensure a smooth transition. We observe newspaper editors advocating extreme stances for their own political reasons; and individuals expressing views with little regard for the consequences of their actions with no sense of responsibility to find solutions.

The desire to blame others is alive and well. We regularly see examples of pandering to particular interests through advocating positions from which compromise becomes almost impossible. We can feel overwhelmed by the fashion of always seeking to attribute blame to others. Too often blaming others is used as a justification for failing to take responsibility for our own responses, as well as an excuse for an inadequate understanding of the constraints on other people.

Nelson Mandela's autobiography, *Long Walk to Freedom*, is a testimony to the practical search for freedom alongside responsible advocacy. This balance of freedom and responsibility was evident in Nelson Mandela's presidency and his focus on reconciliation. A valuable way of assessing any leader is to consider how they use freedom constructively alongside applying a strong sense of both corporate and individual responsibility.

Themes of freedom and responsibility flow throughout the Judeo-Christian tradition. The Psalmist talks about 'freeing me from anguish and setting my heart free'. The focus in John's Gospel is on the Gospel setting people free. The theme of responsibility is central to the teachings of Jesus through the parables. Jesus talks about this generation being responsible for its actions. Paul develops the theme of each person being responsible to God in Corinthians. James talks about perfect law bringing freedom. Leaders influenced by the Christian tradition keep coming back to the balance between freedom and responsibility. Martin Luther, in his book *Three Treaties: the freedom of a Christian*, explores the paradox of freedom and responsibility. He writes, 'the Christian is perfectly free and lord of all, subject to none. A Christian is a perfectly dutiful servant to all.'

Pertinent questions to ask ourselves:

- What freedoms are important to me and why?
- What types of constraints on my freedom are necessary?
- What internal beliefs do I need to be free from in order to make the contributions I want to make going forward?
- What type of responsibilities do I need or want to embrace?
- How might I handle situations where I am reluctant to accept responsibility?
- How do I balance freedom and responsibility in different areas of my life and enable others to find their own equilibrium?

In this short book I explore some aspects of changing contexts and then reflect on what embracing freedom means in different situations. We will look at living out responsibility in ways that are sustainable, and then consider how best to balance freedom and responsibility before looking at some practical next steps. Each chapter concludes with some points for reflection so that the book can be used by both individuals and groups.

As a means of bringing life to the themes in the book I explore the ideas through the leadership journeys of six characters. These are hypothetical individuals drawn from my observations about the challenges leaders face in different spheres. These characters are:

Mary: a senior civil servant
John: a chief operating officer in a big hospital
Bob: a leader of a church
Rachel: a dean of a university department
Geoff: a manager of a local supermarket
Jean: a strategy director at a charity

I have chosen these examples as they represent a range of sectors: namely the public, private, university, charity and church worlds. The issues that leaders face in each of these sectors have many parallels. My hope is that you will identify with some of their stories as you think through how you might use your freedoms in ways which will enable you to live out your values and to have an impact which is consistent with your being at your best in a range of different situations.

Peter Shaw
Godalming, England

Section A

The Changing Context

In this section we look at the expectations on leaders in the modern world, the limits we put on our leadership and our mindset towards freedom and responsibility. We set out some of the dilemmas that leaders face through the experiences of the six characters with whom we are journeying in this book.

1

Expectations on Leaders in the Modern World

We live in a world where communication is fast and furious. We have a huge appetite to receive the latest information. Many of us are addicted to instant communication and news. We feel bereft if we have not looked at the news feed in the last hour. We are constantly irritated by what we read and yet unable to cut ourselves off from the barrage of opinions that are thrust at us.

Leaders face a welter of opinions with solid evidence often being difficult or impossible to establish. We live in a society where many people think that if they shout loudly, and join up with others with a similar single-minded approach, they will get their own way.

We live in a world where customers are fickle and constantly change their views and opinions. Loyalty is regarded as a weakness and not a strength. Often organizations seem more concerned about damaging the reputation of their competitors than refining what they provide to meet the needs of customers.

All leaders are under constant pressure to perform. The relentless focus on results pushes behaviours in ways that are not always constructive. When targets are not met or crises happen, conscientious leaders often find themselves scapegoated rather than given the opportunity to find a sustainable way forward. Performance measures can promote responsibility for delivering outcomes, but they can also erode personal responsibility for finding the most appropriate next steps when uncertainties need to be conscientiously and thoroughly addressed.

The fast pace of information flow and the ability to

communicate with people electronically, 24 hours a day, on the one hand produces a relentless pressure on leaders to be readily available. On the other hand, the focus on wellbeing and the importance of family life creates a pressure on leaders to not allow themselves to be dominated by work. Many people find these two sets of expectations difficult to reconcile, causing an increase in mental health pressures on leaders who can find it difficult to establish an equilibrium which holds true in both work and home situations.

Mary, as a senior civil servant, is expected to be completely committed to delivering the policies of the Government in power. Mary recognizes that this is the basis on which she is employed. She has seen some colleagues fall out of favour because of their loyalty to previous politicians who have moved on. Mary has two lively children and needs to manage her time carefully. The politicians she is working for are hyperactive and can appear dismissive about her restricted availability at the start or the end of the day. She works far longer hours than she is technically employed for and does so because she finds the work stimulating. She finds the constant desire of Ministers and Special Advisors for information on short-term details an inhibitor to the longer-term, strategic planning that is supposedly part of her role. Mary feels pulled in a number of different directions and has to make rapid decisions about how she focuses her energy.

John, as a hospital Chief Operating Officer, feels stuck in the middle of a welter of different expectations. The hospital is expected to perform better. There is a constant risk of public humiliation through the media. John has to address the fear in people's minds that the Health Service Inspectorate is only looking to find problems and will always want to put the knife in. John feels equally battered by the views of medical, nursing and administrative staff who feel hard done by. John's constant plea is that different groups work together more effectively within the hospital, but he is constantly having to contend with out-dated perspectives and unhelpful behaviours from members of different groups within the hospital.

Bob, as a church leader, feels under constant pressure from members of his church to magically produce a way forward. He is assumed to have supernatural authority in persuading people to change their behaviours, or raise significant funds, or increase church attendance. He is expected to be a brilliant ambassador, organizer, pastor, preacher, mentor and fundraiser. No imperfections are allowed.

Rachel, as a university dean, is dealing with colleagues who always think they know best and who expect their individual area to be the top priority. She has to cope with academics who are more interested in their own research than the wellbeing of the university. They might write learned articles but can be curt and rude when seeking to communicate with colleagues. Rachel is expected to produce new cohorts of enthusiastic students each year, while relentless time pressures mean that she has had to give up on some of her own academic interests.

Geoff, as the manager of a large supermarket, is under constant scrutiny. The sales results from his store are available every day. He cannot escape the relentless stream of data about sales in his store. Setting out reasons why sales have fallen cuts no ice with his bosses. Either sales have to improve or he needs to reduce expenditure. He recognizes that his future employment depends on whether he can motivate staff and present the store in such a way that sales increase. If he responds by saying that falling sales are the result of falling incomes in the area or increased competition, Geoff is told that this is his problem to solve.

Jean has a strong sense of vocation, working as the strategy director for a national charity, but recognizes that the finances are precarious. The work of the charity is dependent on the income it receives. Her bright ideas about future strategy are met with responses like, 'how can we possibly afford such a risky approach?' or, 'is it fair on our donors to try out an idea that might not work?' or, 'can we justify an initiative that may not be sustainable?'

Jean was appointed because of her experience in the commercial sector and was willing to take a significant pay cut when joining the charity, yet her sense of vocation and her financial sacrifice seem to her to be perceived as irrelevant. The expectations on her feel even more acute because of this personal sacrifice. There is no sympathy for her when she points out that the resources available to her are highly constrained.

Each of these individuals face expectations related to delivery, performance, communication, constant availability and perfection. All of them are balancing different work and life priorities and feeling that they are not getting much empathy or sympathy from those they are working for.

They are at risk of feeling stuck, and weighed down by responsibility. Pertinent questions for them would relate to the degree of freedom they have going forward and how best to engage with, and not be overwhelmed by, their responsibilities.

Questions for reflection

1 What are the biggest expectations on you as a leader currently and to what extent are they becoming more acute?

2 Are there parallels for you with the experiences of these six characters?

3 How much are you at risk of being overwhelmed by the expectations on you?

2

The Pressures and Limits We Put on Our Own Leadership

The pressures we put on ourselves as leaders can box us in and drain our resolve and energy. Pressures and expectations can also clarify opportunities and give us a focus on a particular outcome, leading into behaviours and results that build our track record and self-esteem. Expectations are not always bad. We need to be clear on what should be the focus of our attention. A strong sense of priority gives us purpose and direction.

Expectations become dangerous when they are unachievable, with no allowance made for the detrimental impact on other areas of our work and life. What can be equally detrimental, however, are the limits we ourselves put on our leadership. We can allow ourselves to be defined by outdated descriptions of our leadership. We can be caught in excessive loyalty to past assumptions and leaders. We can be gripped with apprehension and anxieties about risks and uncertainties. We can be fearful of different situations without understanding why.

We can be caught within assumptions inherited from our parents. We can assume, too easily, that we lack the expertise and insight to move beyond our current comfort zones. We can put excessive limitations upon our own potential because of personal and professional inhibitions. We can allow personal prejudices to hold us back. There can be a fear of the unknown or a fear of getting into trouble or conflict that means we don't explore leadership opportunities to which we might be suited. Criticism we once received can still circulate in our heads and be a repeated voice of disdain or caution. We hate the prospect of failure and, therefore, are reluctant to go near opportunities that might bring out qualities in us that are latent rather than obvious.

What could have held Mary back was her deference to Government Ministers. She had observed Ministers apparently scapegoating officials whom Ministers had felt were not fully committed to them. She was hesitant to show any disagreement with a Minister. Speaking truth to power was something that was an anathema to her. Mary wanted to be liked and respected by Ministers for doing a good job. She recognized that this inhibition could hold her back in the long term, but she was not willing to risk her reputation by pushing back if she felt a Minister was taking an inappropriate course of action.

John respected the Chief Executive of the hospital where he was the Chief Operating Officer. He always wanted to know the CEO's view on particular issues before he was willing to take action. A consequence was that sometimes John could appear indecisive because he was at risk of waiting for a definitive answer. John recognized that he was reluctant to use the freedom he had in his role to make decisions because of this sense of deference to the Chief Executive. As he did not want to make a mistake he was over-reliant on the lead from his CEO.

John recognized that he needed to be more willing to use the freedoms he had and make decisions and accept the likelihood of making some mistakes. He recognized that sometimes it was right to seek forgiveness after the event rather than permission in advance of making a decision.

Bob was conscious that members of the church council had a lot more experience than he did. He was concerned not to offend people who were older than him, whom he respected as they brought lots of experience of leadership within the church and the wider community. The consequence was that Bob would often hold his own views back and dismiss them without talking them through with others because he felt they would disapprove of his ideas.

Bob was learning that he needed to explore ideas in an open way with senior church members. There was a consensus about the broad direction for the church over the next few years with Bob operating within an agreed framework. But he recognized that the fear of disapproval or rejection was limiting his willingness to talk ideas through in an open and constructive way. He recognized that he needed to be less fearful of the reactions from people he respected and more willing to allow his ideas to be shaped by others.

Rachel had always enjoyed her academic research and her work with students. She revelled in dialogue with her students and was at her most animated in discussing research topics with doctoral candidates. When she became the departmental dean she was looking forward to the status, but had not fully appreciated how much committee work she would need to do. She found her initial enthusiasm was continually squashed by her hesitation in meetings with colleagues. She needed to make her mark on behalf of her department and be part of the corporate leadership but felt this was not her preference and not the reason she was working at a university.

Rachel knew she had to get over this inhibition. She recognized that the dean's role required her to take a significant part in the corporate leadership. This was not an optional extra. It was central to her success and that of the university. Rachel's anxieties about her role in corporate leadership were inhibiting her freedom to contribute and meant that she was not fulfilling her responsibilities as a senior leader. Rachel recognized that there needed to be a change in her approach.

Geoff felt completely responsible for the performance of the supermarket he managed. His strong sense of personal responsibility had been a valuable asset in his career so far. He had managed individual departments with energy and been a trailblazer in introducing new ideas. Head office had viewed him as someone with high potential because of his energy and his personal sense of responsibility in delivering whatever he was asked to do.

Geoff had found the step change to become a store manager uncomfortable. His personal sense of responsibility meant that he felt an overriding duty to deliver success in every area. The consequence was that Geoff was not using his team in a forward-looking way: they were operatives given specific jobs to do. He was not drawing out ideas and initiatives from his team who, as a consequence, were not particularly motivated to develop their leadership potential within the store.

Geoff began to recognize that his strong sense of individual responsibility was getting in the way of his effective leadership of the wider team. He knew he had to make a change in the way he engaged with people within his organization and address his over-developed sense of personal responsibility.

Jean found the transition from the commercial sector to the charity sector to be more difficult than she had anticipated. She oscillated between wanting to share her insights from the commercial sector and being inhibited by a very different culture and language within the charity world. She found the charity trustees to be quite narrow-minded and as a result she tended to keep quiet because she did not want to irritate them or be irritated by them. The charity's CEO recognized that Jean brought a lot of insight from the commercial world and was deliberate in encouraging Jean to share those insights.

Jean had to get over both her hesitation about sharing insights from a different world and the potential resentment that could well up in her if she felt that the trustees and other colleagues were dismissive of her background and contributions.

These six individuals bring a range of different self-limiting assumptions. They have begun to recognize the limits they are putting on their own leadership but are at risk of not responding as constructively as they might because of the risk of disappointment, frustration or criticism.

Questions for reflection

1 What resonates most from these examples about limitations you might be putting on your own leadership?

2 What are the self-limiting assumptions that might be affecting you?

3 What steps can you take to break down those assumptions?

4 How close are you to moving constructively through self-limiting assumptions into a more positive place?

3

Our Mindset Towards Freedom and Responsibility

Is our current frame of mind inclined towards choices that increase our freedom or reduce freedom? Is our tendency to accept responsibility or move away from situations where we may be invited to take on responsibility? Both stances are potentially unhelpful and can be dangerous. Restricting our freedom too much means we do not try new things and do not develop the potential that is within us. Using our freedom to get involved in a wide range of different options at the same time can dilute our impact and stunt our growth as individuals and leaders. Too little responsibility and we stay in a limited and myopic world. Taking on an excess of responsibility can leave us exhausted and let down those people who are closest to us.

Three words that might influence our mindset are clarity, consistency and compromise. As an illustration of seeking clarity, one of my objectives in coaching conversations is to enable an individual or team to be clearer about their freedom of action and how they are linking together their different responsibilities. My objective is to enable people to keep reshaping their clarity of understanding about their priorities and their scope for freedom of action within the mix of responsibilities that they are holding together.

My aim is to encourage individuals and teams to relish and use the freedoms that they have, while recognizing the constraints they are operating under. I want to help them see their responsibilities as key to delivering the overall purpose and impact of the organization they are part of. The mindset that I am seeking to help develop is about a positive approach to walking towards problems rather than moving away from them. Part of seeking clarity is enabling people to be clearer about the key questions that need to be addressed, the people that need to be influenced and the variables that they need to be conscious of.

Consistency relates both to personal equilibrium, in terms of a consistent frame of mind, and to reputation and respect, whereby others see us as consistent in our leadership approach while also taking account of changing circumstances. Priorities change in the light of new information and circumstances, but a consistency of values and attitudes helps maintain personal integrity and allows others to see the pattern in your perspectives and actions and respect what you are seeking to achieve.

Portsmouth in New Hampshire was the scene of the first skirmish in the American War of Independence. It was also where a group of black slaves submitted a petition to the New Hampshire Government in 1779 about their freedom. The slaves were making the point that the newly independent America, now enjoying its freedom, should bring a consistent belief in freedom and be willing to give freedom to the slaves. In this petition they wrote:

> Therefore, your humble slaves most devotedly pray for the sake of injured liberty; for the sake of justice, humanity and the rights of mankind; the honour of religion; and by all that is dear, that your honours would graciously interpose on our behalf and enact such laws and regulations as you in your wisdom think proper, whereby we may regain our liberty and be ranked in the class of free agents and that the name of slave may not more be heard in the land gloriously contending for the sweets of freedom.

This illustration from New Hampshire is a historic example of a lack of consistency as the Americans sought their own freedom but did not want to give freedom to the slaves. All of us live with inconsistencies. What matters is that we do not delude ourselves and believe we are being consistent when we are patently not.

Compromises are often required, as balancing freedom and responsibility is not straightforward. We may balance things in different ways at different stages. When family responsibilities are particularly acute we will probably not readily volunteer to take on further responsibilities at work or in the community. There will be moments when we limit our responsibilities in particular ways and say no to different freedoms as a deliberate choice. What is important is that we bring a mindset of recognizing the importance of compromise as an appropriate and sustainable way forward in many situations.

In her last substantive speech as Prime Minister in July 2019, Theresa May delivered an address on the state of politics at Chatham House. She was speaking at a time when Brexit discussions were at their most intense but her comments have much wider applicability. Theresa May talked about the willingness to compromise having become unfashionable. She was deliberate in saying she was not talking about compromising on values; nor did she mean accepting the lowest common denominator or clinging to outmoded ideas out of apathy or fear. She reinforced the importance of being driven by, and when necessary standing up for, values and convictions. She emphasized that standing up for values and convictions needs to be done in the real world where others are making their own case and pursuing their own interests. She said:

Persuasion, teamwork and a willingness to make mutual concessions are needed to achieve an optimal outcome. That is politics at its best. The alternative is a politics of winners and losers and perpetual strife and that threatens us all. Today an inability to combine principles with pragmatism and make a compromise when required seems to have driven our whole political discourse down the wrong path. It has led to what is in effect a form of 'absolutism' – one which believes that if you simply assert your view loud enough and long enough you will get your way in the end. Or that mobilising your own faction is more important than bringing others with you.

This is coarsening our public debate. Some are losing the ability to disagree without demeaning the view of others. On-line technology allows people to express their anger and anxiety without filter or accountabilities. Aggressive assertions are made without regard to the facts or the complexities of an issue, in an environment where the most extreme views tend to be the most noticed. The descent of our debate into rancour and tribal business – and in some cases even violent abuse at a criminal level – is corrosive to the democratic values which we should all be seeking to uphold. It risks closing down the space for reasoned debate and subverting the principle of freedom of speech.

These valedictory words from Theresa May as Prime Minister bring home the need to find common ground and be willing to find a way forward that is a genuine compromise which respects difference and does not steamroller people into submission.

We make compromises every day in the way we balance priorities and use our time and energy. A mindset towards freedom and responsibility that respects individual values and cultural histories, while at the same time recognizing the need for compromise, is more likely to build alliances that are sustainable and respected by those whose voices can reinforce or undermine the way forward.

My theory is that, in order to be sustainable, a mindset balancing freedom and responsibility needs to bring together:

- clarity of thinking about intent, priorities and the perspectives of others
- consistency in the application of values and communication
- compromise in the light of realities, seeking a common purpose and partnerships which increase the likelihood of a sustainable outcome.

Questions for reflection

1 Does your natural mindset embrace both freedom and responsibility or walk away from freedom and responsibility?

2 How much clarity do you currently apply in the way you balance freedom and responsibility?

3 To what extent is your approach consistent in different areas of your life? Where it is not consistent; are there good reasons for this inconsistency?

4 How willing are you to compromise in the way you use your freedom and accept responsibility, and what tests do you apply to your decisions when you compromise?

Section B

Embracing Freedom

In this section we look at what embracing freedom means for leaders in different contexts. We start with recognizing our own freedoms and understanding the inhibitions that constrain us and then move into distinguishing between 'freedom from' and 'freedom to'. We look at pushing the boundaries to explore new-found freedom, and accepting limitations around our freedom. We reflect on using the freedom to say 'no' with a smile, and then explore how best to enable others to grow in exercising their own freedoms.

4

Recognize Your Own Freedoms and Understand the Inhibitions which Constrain You

We often feel that our freedoms are markedly constrained by rules, policies and expected norms. It can often feel that we are bounded by constraints and have little choice, but our freedoms may be much greater than we sometimes allow ourselves to believe. We may have clear objectives to deliver, but for most leaders planning how their time is spent is, to a large extent, at the discretion of the individual.

Every morning a leader is making choices about their attitude to the day, their demeanour with others, the words they use and the signals they give. The diary may feel constrained. There may be tasks that need to be completed or people pressing to have a conversation. The 'what' of the day may feel constrained but there may be more scope in terms of 'how' the day is to be approached.

When a colleague is unsure about their next action you may choose to go into directive mode and be clear about the next steps that are required, or you may choose to go into coaching mode and enable the individual to work through their own thoughts about next steps. You may feel your freedom is constrained by the long list of tasks that need to be done, but there is often the freedom to decide in which order you tackle them and how much you might seek to involve others before making a final decision.

Your boss may set clear expectations that a submission is

with them by a particular time, but you have the discretion to decide how you put a proposal together and how you shape key components. You may feel stuck in a classroom with a group of students for three hours with a topic that is required to be addressed, but you have the discretion to decide how you present the key themes and to what extent you are in lecture mode or create stimulating interactions in the classroom.

Recognizing your freedom as a leader does not mean ignoring factors that constrain your freedom. If the budget total is fixed or you are operating within declared published policies, your room for manoeuvre is inevitably constrained. Some of the limitations may frustrate you, and there may be a future occasion when those constraints can be challenged, but you recognize that realism needs to reign on a day-to-day basis with choices made within a set of constraints that are there for particular reasons and cannot be ignored or changed overnight.

Sometimes boundaries that constrain are external ones: on other occasions inhibitions are self-inflicted boundaries that constrain, because you decide to limit your own choices. You do not have the discretion to spend money that is not within your control. You cannot change policies or procedures that are outside your discretionary responsibilities. Your boss carries the ultimate accountability and, therefore, you cannot make their decisions for them. In recognizing your freedoms, you have to start from understanding the constraints that inevitably limit your discretion.

Geoff as a manager of a big supermarket often felt overwhelmed by pressures from Head Office. There was a relentless procession of requirements. Geoff knew he was perceived as a big personality. If he was feeling grumpy that grumpiness could transmit itself through the whole supermarket. On the other hand, there were options available to the head of a big supermarket in terms of some product lines and supermarket layouts. He had authority over recruitment and promotion, with a degree of independence in terms of bonuses and working patterns.

In addition Geoff recognized he had the freedom to enthuse and motivate. He was good at recognizing potential and giving people additional responsibility, but he recognized that he needed to be deliberate in passing responsibility to others which was not always straightforward, because of his strong sense of personal responsibility.

As he drove to the supermarket each day, he was deliberate in thinking about what his demeanour was going to be as he entered the supermarket and how he was going to communicate with people on that day. To what extent would he be walking around the store meeting staff and seeking to be aware of how customers were responding to different marketing approaches? He was conscious that he set a tone on staff behaviours which demonstrated that he was willing to be tough where trust was being abused.

Geoff knew that he needed to be compassionate when the personal circumstances of staff members meant that they needed some flexibility in the hours they worked. Geoff was aware that he set a clear tone on how theft was tackled and how inappropriate behaviour in relation to staff was dealt with. When Geoff felt constrained by the myriad of requests from Head Office, he kept telling himself that there were still considerable areas of freedom in the way he led the organization that made a significant difference to the experience of both staff and customers.

In one sense Bob, as a church leader, has far greater freedom than most leaders. The only times when he has to turn up are for the church services on a Sunday. There are many other meetings and services in the diary but these were organized largely by him with a considerable degree of freedom in his decisions about the pattern of his working week. When speaking in the pulpit he could be seen as 'six foot above contradiction'. There was an annual visitation from the Archdeacon. The Bishop would come when invited to special events, but Bob did not experience the same mass of written instructions as did other leaders.

Bob was mindful of the guidance of Paul to the Galatians that, 'it is for freedom that Christ has set us free. Stand firm, then, and do not let yourselves be burdened again by the yoke of slavery ... You, my brothers and sisters were called to be free, but do not use your freedom to indulge your sinful nature; rather serve one another humbly in love.'

Bob recognized that he had the freedom to serve others in the church and wider community. This gave him choices about how to use his time. This freedom brought risks as he could be highly selective about who he spent time with and could either work excessive hours or fritter away time rather than use it constructively. Bob needed to stand back every so often and think carefully about how he used his freedom in the time available to him. There were a couple of key people within his church community with whom he had regular conversations in order to hear their perspective and to reassess how he kept reprioritizing his time in the light of changed circumstances.

Questions for reflection

1 What are the freedoms that are most precious to you in your current role?

2 How fully do you deploy the freedoms that are available to you?

3 How best do you shape your thinking each day on how you are going to apply the freedoms available to you?

5

Distinguish Between 'Freedom From' and 'Freedom To'

There is a danger that we become obsessed with feeling constrained in what we have the 'freedom to' do and take for granted a lot of the things we have 'freedom from'. When we have freedom from hunger, poverty, violence, extortion and persecution we can take those freedoms for granted. Previous generations have worked hard to ensure freedom from oppression, extortion, abuse and segregation. These 'freedoms from' have been developed over centuries and are precious in any civilized society, but these 'freedoms from' cannot be taken for granted. A spate of knife killings in a city and sporadic acts of terrorism can be painful reminders that freedoms are fragile, with the need for constant vigilance as to when they are at risk of being eroded.

I remember taking my sons to some premier league football games and being appalled by the use of violent and abusive language from some spectators about the football players. It reminded me that abuse is just below the surface and can erupt too readily. In that situation I did not feel I could say anything about the abusive use of language by those spectators as their violence might then have been directed at me.

As a leader you want to create a context where your staff have the freedom to use their experience and insights to best effect, with freedom from unreasonable interference or inappropriate behaviour. You want to create a positive forward-looking approach where 'freedoms to' are embraced with enthusiasm alongside a desire to learn and push the limits of previous practice and understanding. You are seeking to keep a careful eye on what might inhibit and destroy freedoms with the resulting risk of over-cautious and negative behaviour.

John felt that the performance of the hospital where he was the Chief Operating Officer was continually under review. He felt that his personal reputation was dependent on the success of the hospital in terms of the throughput of patients and the number of operations. John recognized that one performance measure not being met would not result in his immediate exit. His physical security was not dependent on what happened in the hospital.

On the other hand John knew that if there were a succession of problems in the effective operational running of the hospital that his long-term prospects at the hospital would be diminished. He recognized that he would not be dismissed at a moment's notice nor would there be a public flogging. While John knew that he was working in a country where he would not suffer physical humiliation he was conscious that he could be subject to mental humiliation.

John had observed people in his profession in other hospitals under constant verbal attack in the media, which had led to unproductive working relationships, short-term decision-making and ill-thought-through actions that had gone wrong. The accumulation of errors and short-term decision-making led to a growth in anxiety among individuals, ill-tempered engagement in so-called teams, and destructive working environments that undermined confidence and heightened anxieties.

John recognized that he needed to protect his people from the threat of verbal abuse by those determined to humiliate those seeking to run the hospital responsibly. John fully recognized that the Health Inspectorate needed to be treated with respect and he sought to build constructive relationships with individuals in the Health Regulatory Bodies, fully respecting their freedom to report responsibly. John recognized that hospital staff and inspectors could feel distrusted and abused by their opposite numbers. John sought to build an atmosphere of trust which ensured there was a freedom from unfair criticism and a freedom to explore openly and honestly what had gone well or less well.

After her first six months as Strategy Director in her charity Jean reflected on the balance between 'freedom from' and 'freedom to'. She was relieved to have 'freedom from' relentless commercial expectations, a relentless desire for big profits, egocentric views of her bosses and a persistent excessive enthusiasm. She had come from an organization which had felt oppressive to an organization where there was greater freedom to be authentic and bring your own personality to work. Jean had to keep reminding herself that she was glad to have moved on from her previous organization, which she had found debilitating.

At the same time Jean was wrestling with the frustration of working in an environment where her commercial skills did not seem to be fully appreciated. Jean kept telling herself that she now had the freedom to be fully part of a charitable enterprise. She was not dominated by a profit motive. She did not have to conform to a particular set of normative behaviours, as had been expected within her previous commercial organization. There was a good degree of freedom to discuss ideas and approaches, even though the financial resources were much more limited than in a commercial organization. Jean realized it would take longer to make a significant difference but she was pleased that she had already been able to make a difference in the way the charity was moving forward. There was a freedom to build working relationships with the trustees even though some of their initial ideas seemed to her myopic and caught in an outdated, historic perspective.

Questions for reflection

1 What do you have 'freedoms from' in your current role that you sometimes might take for granted?

2 What freedoms might you be at risk of not recognizing?

3 To what extent is there a risk that you get frustrated by your limited 'freedoms to', when the reality is you have a lot of 'freedoms from' abuse, exploitation, poverty and humiliation?

6

Push the Boundaries to Explore New-found Freedom

When I coach leaders promoted into new roles there are often two phases in the coaching. In the first six months in post, an individual needs to fully recognize and respond to the expectations of the people who appointed them. The newly appointed individual needs to focus their efforts so that they are delivering on expectations and building a reputation for competence.

At the end of six months it is often helpful to have a review point where an individual is able to bank the progress they have made and be conscious of the reputation they have established. This review point becomes a good moment to explore what boundaries might be stretched going forward and where new initiatives could be embarked upon. If a good basis of trust has been established in the first six months, this means that the individual has credibility so that their suggestions are taken seriously. After six months they will have the scope to take forward new ideas without feeling the need to double-check that every opportunity they take forward is sensible.

In the first few months the boss might have taken an interest in how particular steps are taken. After six months the boss may be more willing to allow the individual freedom in how they fulfil the requirements on them, provided the objectives are met. Sometimes a conversation is needed between the individual and the boss to agree this change in working practice so that there is no misunderstanding about how much freedom to act an individual has been given.

At periodic intervals it is worth re-examining assumptions about the limitations on the scope for action. Some of those limitations might be historic and worth questioning. Other apparently innocuous limitations might be there for good reason but even these need to be reassessed from time to time.

When seeking to push the boundaries it is always worth asking yourself who might be annoyed or put out. You might be entering other people's territory without fully realizing that this is what you are doing. Your pushing the boundaries of one freedom might create a consequential restriction in freedom for others. It is worth anticipating such consequences in advance and talking the potential implications through with potentially affected individuals. They may be open to their freedoms being affected provided they know why you are taking the course of action that you have embarked upon.

When you are established in a role you are likely to have the freedom to be involved in a wider range of activities. You may seek to, or be invited to, participate in corporate activities that you find interesting. There may be personal interests or areas of professional development you might want to take forward. There is a risk that exploring new-found freedom might be like being in a sweet shop with such a range of choices that you might be mesmerized by the range or over-indulgent in the number of choices you take forward. When exploring new-found freedoms it is worth revisiting why you are following those freedoms and what you want to learn from taking up those opportunities. When you have new freedom about how to use your time it is worth reflecting on what is core to your role and how success will be measured by those who will determine your future.

Mary was developing policies to implement a manifesto commitment. She had been appointed to this role on promotion after a competitive process. The successful implementation of the policy she was working on was key to the Minister's success. Mary knew she had good levels of support from junior members of the Department and had access to a reasonable financial budget. Initially she had felt a little inhibited as a member of the Senior Civil Service, which accentuated the risk of her being too deferential to more senior people. Prompted by her mentor, Mary recognized that she needed to be more assertive in expressing her views and in seeking the backing and support of people across the Department. Her boss was firm that she had every reason to speak up forcefully in meetings.

As a member of the Senior Civil Service she had responsibility to deliver a policy, alongside the freedom to speak truth and say what obstacles needed to be overcome for the policy to be delivered effectively. Mary became less inhibited in saying what she thought in meetings: she knew she needed to be clear, crisp and concise. Mary knew she needed to build allies before meetings and develop a strong sense of common purpose with colleagues who had agendas which interacted with hers. Mary recognized that she needed to relax into the freedom that this role gave her. She did not need to be dogmatic: if she was dogmatic it would count against her. What mattered was that she deployed the evidence she had available clearly and persuasively, so that there was clarity about the consequences and potential courses of action.

After six months in this leadership role Mary offered to take on a couple of corporate responsibilities which were time-consuming but added to her enjoyment and learning in the role. She had joined a committee looking at career progression for disabled people and she became a member of a promotion board. Both of these wider responsibilities were developing her confidence and the ease with which she could express views drawn from the breadth of her experience.

After her first few months as the dean of a university department Rachel felt worn down by the weight of her responsibilities. She felt a weight of responsibility to the university senior executive team for the success of the academic department, and to the senior colleagues in her department for gaining resources from university funding streams. She felt caught in the middle and feared that both the university senior executive team and her staff were viewing her critically. Rachel was desperate to build her reputation upwards, downwards and sideways. She was not at ease with herself and felt uncomfortable in this leadership role where she had to face so many directions at the same time.

Rachel accepted that her current attitude was unsustainable. She had to reach a point where she turned what felt like aggravations into opportunities. She needed to stop feeling frustrated and sorry for herself. She needed to be clearer about how she was going to split her time and what her priorities were going to be going forward. She knew she had to build a stronger relationship with her fellow deans and the pro vice chancellor to whom she reported. Rachel needed to turn up at the meetings of the deans in a constructive rather than a negative frame of mind. She recognized that she needed to take the initiative sometimes in suggesting what the deans might focus on and how they could contribute to the best use of funding at the university and to the more effective recruitment of students.

Rachel was required to spend less time with students and, therefore, had more discretion in the use of her time: she told herself that she should see this greater freedom in the use of her time as a plus and stop feeling overwhelmed by the inbox. She had to accept what was unavoidable in terms of her responsibilities, her participation in key conversations and the need to be more deliberate in shaping how she used her time and energy. After giving herself a good talking to, she resolved to be less sorry for herself and to see opportunities where previously she had seen burdens.

Questions for reflection

1 What are the boundaries to the freedom you have in your current role which need to be reassessed?

2 What freedoms do you have in your role which you could take to another level?

3 How do you balance and keep within reasonable bounds the range of freedoms that you have in your current role?

4 How do you ensure that you do not follow up on too many opportunities in a way that detracts from the delivery of what is core to your role?

5 How do you decide which boundaries to push and where to accept the current limitations upon you?

7

Accept Limitations Around Your Freedom

In many areas of our life we accept limitations around our freedom. We recognize why we need to drive a car with care and why we should only walk across the road after having checked that there is no traffic coming. We accept that the use of electronic communications means that there need to be new boundaries around personal freedom. We recognize that we can only contact people regularly electronically if we have their agreement to do so.

We like the freedom to express our views and may welcome the opportunity to have a wider audience through social media. We are increasingly cognizant of the damaging effect of the misuse of social media. A range of organizations have introduced social media community guidelines. As an illustration of good practice, the following are the guidelines introduced by the Church of England in 2019:

- **Be safe**. The safety of children, young people and vulnerable adults must be maintained.
- **Be respectful.** Do not post or share content that is sexually explicit, inflammatory, hateful, abusive, threatening or otherwise disrespectful.
- **Be kind**. Treat others how you would wish to be treated and assume the best in people. If you have criticism or critique to make, consider not just whether you would say it in person, but the tone you would use.
- **Be honest**. Don't mislead people about who you are.

- **Take responsibility**. You are accountable for the things you do, say and write. Text and images shared can be public and permanent, even with privacy settings in place. If you are not sure, don't post it.
- **Be a good ambassador**. Personal and professional life can easily be blurred online so think before you post
- **Disagree well**. Some conversations can be places of robust disagreement and it is important we apply our own values in the way we express them.
- **Credit others**. Acknowledge the work of others. Respect copyright and always give credit where it is due. Be careful not to release sensitive or confidential information and always question the sources of any content you are considering amplifying.
- **Follow the rules**. Abide by the terms and conditions of the various social media platforms themselves.

As a leader you are being watched all the time. Your views and actions are being megaphoned around the organization. The way you use your freedoms will be followed by others in the organization. If you use your freedom to be critical of the hierarchy above you, then others will feel free to criticize those in the hierarchy above them, that is, you. Seeing yourself as a role model for others in the organization can feel a burden, but also provides a valuable opportunity to influence attitudes and behaviours across the organization.

There may be occasions when you limit your freedom because of the signals it gives to other people. You may have the freedom to work at home on a regular basis and to work the pattern of hours that fits best for you. There may be good operational reasons why it is not appropriate to allow a similar freedom to many of the people working in your organization. There may be occasions when you decide not to use the full scope of the freedoms available to you in order to be very visible to the people working for you. Or you may decide to communicate clearly how you are using the freedom you have in terms of your time and location to people in the organization, recognizing that it is not realistic for many of the other people in the organization to have the same freedoms as those available to you.

There are some limitations around the freedom in any job which are an inevitable consequence of the role. If you are working for a university it would not be personally or professionally sensible to be highly critical publicly of that university. If you work for one commercial organization and decide that you would like the freedom to share that organization's secrets with a competitor then your actions will not be welcomed by your employer who rightly will regard your actions as an irresponsible breach of trust.

Mary knew as a senior civil servant that it would not be appropriate for her to express disagreement publicly with the policies of the Government for whom she was working. She could not speak up in support of policies that were contrary to those she was developing or implementing for the current Government. Mary did keep abreast of the thinking and action of a range of groups in the policy area that she was leading. She kept her ears open to what people were saying.

Mary was not blinkered to different approaches or evidence. If she felt the Minister was going down the wrong track she recognized that she had a responsibility to point out relevant evidence to the Minister, but she knew she needed to do this within the relationship of trust and in a way that allowed the Minister to think through the implications of new evidence. The Minister must never feel pressured into premature decisions by her presentation of new data. Mary recognized that when she was at events outside the Department she was there as the ambassador of the Minister and it was for her to set out the views of Ministers. When she was in meetings with Ministers, Mary recognized that her role was to be clear about the facts and implications and be willing to speak 'truth to power' in a way that recognized the concerns of Ministers.

As a church leader Bob recognized that he had far more freedom than others about how he used his time. His sense of vocation was strong and, therefore, he could in principle serve as a church minister seven days a week, 24 hours a day. Bob recognized that his own wellbeing depended on putting some limitations around his freedom, being clear about his day off and how he was going to ensure that this time was protected. Bob recognized that he needed to be aware about what issues his Bishop was addressing. He wanted to be supportive of his Bishop and recognized that it would not be helpful to either of them if he publicly disagreed with him. Therefore, Bob had a self-imposed limitation that he was not going to say anything that was at odds with what the Bishop had been advocating.

Although a church minister is a free agent in the way time is used, Bob was clear that he wanted his use of time to be within a framework agreed by his parish council. There were two key lay people who were senior members of the church (the two churchwardens) with whom Bob met on a regular basis. He was clear that he wanted to act in accord with what he and the wardens jointly deemed to be the key priorities. He was willing to put a limitation around the use of his freedom in order to focus on these priorities.

Limitations around your freedom may be for a season. You may have decided that you will not explore other work possibilities until you have been in the current role for a specific period of time. You may have deliberately curtailed your freedom to look for other roles for thought-through reasons. Then after a defined period of, say, a couple of years, you may conclude that now is the moment to explore other possibilities. Constraining your freedom for a period of time might have been helpful in allowing you to think subsequently in a fresh way about future job opportunities.

Questions for reflection

1 How constrained do you currently feel by limitations you have placed around your freedom in your current role?

2 How do you identify those limitations which are transitory and those that should be permanent?

3 When do you want to leap for joy because a limitation on your freedom has been reduced?

4 How frequently is it worth reviewing the balance between the time and energy you use on core activities and the time you devote to opportunities beyond the core?

8

Say 'No' with a Smile

After 32 years as a civil servant working for the UK Government, I moved into executive coaching and was beginning to build up a portfolio of clients. I was approached by the Permanent Secretary of a government department and asked if I would consider leading a disciplinary inquiry. I felt honoured to have been asked as it was an acknowledgement of the type of contribution I had made as a senior civil servant, but I was delighted to say 'no' to this request. Having the freedom to say no felt like an emancipation. I had spent 32 years doing whatever a Permanent Secretary asked me to do: it was a liberation to be able to say 'no' and turn down the request. The fact that I made this decision so readily was confirmation to me that I had made the right choice to move into a second career of executive coaching.

Having worked for so long in the public sector there has been considerable freedom in working in the private sector. I am able to say 'no' if I do not think that I am best suited to work with a particular client, individual or team. I can say 'no' when I think that there are unreasonable expectations from an organization or individual about what will come out of coaching conversations.

The freedom to say 'no' is something every leader needs to keep hold of. If you always feel you have to say 'yes' to any request from a boss, client or customer then your values may be sorely tested and your energy and credibility dissipated. Every leader will experience some situations where they feel they are being asked to do something unreasonable, or complete a task on an unreasonable timescale. A categorical, 'no, I can't do that' is likely to be met with an equally obstructive response. Years of working with Government Ministers taught me that when you are asked to do something unreasonable you can respond with an alternative proposal that delivers, as closely as possible, what the Minister has requested. Many a leader will start off making an initial request that is unreasonable in order to get to an outcome that is as close as possible to their ideal result, hence the importance of not being brow-beaten into submission, but thinking through what is possible and then setting out, with clear evidence, what can be done on different timescales.

Saying 'no' with a smile can be misinterpreted if the smile is one of sarcasm, disdain or looks churlish and self-satisfied. The fixed grin when saying 'no' is not likely to receive a warm, receptive response. Saying 'no' with a smile works best when a relationship has been established based on trust and mutual understanding. Megaphone diplomacy expressed through Twitter quotes or soundbite messages is unlikely to produce that sense of shared journey and rapport in which honest conversations can consider alternative ways forward.

Part of the art of saying 'no' is to depersonalize the response. You can say 'no' more readily when there is a clear policy that informs the answer, for example a decision has been made by a governance group, or a decision is a joint one with other key people. Sometimes you want the freedom to make your own decisions but often order and consistency is best maintained in an organization if individual freedom is subject to collective policies or decision-making which restricts the scope for someone to be put into the position where they feel isolated when always having to say 'no'.

John felt bombarded by requests from medical consultants about resources. They always seemed to have a special, unique situation, arguing that their case was unique and different to any others. John had become immune to the emotional arguments used to try to persuade him, but he did find it emotionally draining when one medical consultant after another came to press him for special treatment. John learnt early on that he needed to work closely with the Medical Director, who had the ultimate accountability for decisions that related to medical matters. John invested a lot of time in his working relationship with the Medical Director to seek to ensure that they were at one when decisions needed to be made on resourcing and were able to talk through cases in an open and dispassionate way.

When John was in conversation with individual medical consultants he would either talk through the issue first with the Medical Director or would anticipate the Medical Director's perspective. He was confident when he said 'no' that he would not be undermined, hence he could say 'no' in a way that maintained a good working relationship with the medical consultants. If a medical consultant became overly assertive or hostile with John, or sent e-mails in capital letters after he had said 'no', John did not respond in an aggressive way. He responded clearly and simply that he had looked at the evidence and was not in a position to respond to the request. Over time the senior medical staff came to appreciate that John would look at cases carefully but would reach his own decision and was not going to be pressured into changing his mind through the use of excessive emotional language.

John knew he had to prepare carefully for meetings of the Board of the Hospital Trust where he would be expected to explain carefully decisions that had been made and respond thoughtfully to suggestions from the Trust members. John knew that he had to be on top of his brief for such meetings so that when he was explaining that something was not possible, he was setting out clear reasons. John also recognized that because of the experience of the Trust members, they might well be making good points which he needed to think further about before he gave a definitive answer.

Geoff in his role as a supermarket manager was forever having to strengthen the resolve of his team to say 'no'. It felt as if there was constant pleading from staff for special treatment;

for example, some staff did not like working with certain people and wanted to move around and do different shifts. They all seemed to want holidays at the same time. The suppliers wanted to change some of their routines, which would inconvenience other members of staff.

Geoff wanted his senior staff to be supportive where appropriate in their decisions, but the risk was that any concession would be assumed to be the new norm. The supermarket existed for the benefit of customers and not the staff who worked there. In a firm but polite way he wanted to ensure his senior staff were willing to say 'no' when repeated requests were made which, if they were all implemented, would mean the store failing to serve its customers effectively.

While Geoff understood the phrase 'the customer is always right', he recognized that not all customers behave in a responsible way. Some would keep complaining about minor things. Others would be blatantly dishonest. Some would be rude to his staff. Geoff recognized that he and his senior staff would sometimes need to say 'no', firmly and dispassionately, to customers who were bending the rules. Geoff knew that through any altercation he needed to keep calm and be consistent in saying 'no' based on clear evidence.

Questions for reflection

1 When do you feel obligated to say 'yes' to all requests?

2 What helps you say 'no' in a confident and convincing way?

3 What can get in the way of your saying 'no' when you know that is the right answer?

4 How best do you say 'no' with a smile?

9

Enable Others to Grow in Exercising Their Freedom

Responsible parenting involves developing in children the capacity to use freedom responsibly. At age three it is about how they eat responsibly, at age eight it is about their responsibility to choose which books to read or decide what programmes to look at on television, while at age 15 it is about choosing their friends and deciding who to engage with on social media.

As a parent you hope that you have helped your children develop a framework for making decisions that keeps them safe and allows them to make decisions that they can live with. You want to help them ensure that they can make decisions without being burdened by them. You try your best to help them recognize constraints on their freedom and use the opportunities they have in life to make a responsible contribution to the different communities of which they are part.

When the Apostle Paul was writing to the young leader Timothy, he reminded Timothy that 'the Spirit God gave us does not make us timid, but gives us power, love and self-discipline'. This is wise advice from any leader to a protégé. Paul was reminding Timothy of the authority he had as a young leader, the importance of bringing a compassionate approach in all his decisions, and the need for self-discipline in using his time and energy well.

One of the joys of leadership is developing the next generation. Developing your succession is part of the duty of any leader so that there is an effective choice about who will take an organization into the next phase of its journey. Helping others grow in exercising their freedom requires an ability to let go and let others have the privilege and responsibility of leadership. On the basis that often the most effective learning comes from experiences that don't go well, developing the next generation of leaders includes allowing them to take risks and produce results that may not meet our exacting standards. All of us learn more from what goes less well than what goes smoothly.

Sometimes the exercise of freedom is best given to a defined group rather than just one or two individuals. In this way, learning about what works well or less well will be shared. Part of the growth of leaders will be to understand where they need to cede control to others. Part of exercising freedom as an emerging leader is about taking responsibility: but it is also about the freedom to allow a group to reach decisions and potentially make their own mistakes.

Rachel, as dean of a university department, was keen for two departments to develop a joint honours programme. She feared that both departments would tend to be territorial in these discussions. She identified a team to work together and gave them a clear remit and timetable. She suspected that their initial efforts would be to piece together existing modules. When such a package was presented to her she was clear that the team needed to think again and exercise a freer spirit in thinking about the type of students who might take this joint honours programme and what outcomes from the programme would best suit the students. The working group had started from the perspective of what was going to be taught rather than what was going to be learnt. Rachel was direct in saying that they needed to go back to first principles and overcome some of their inhibitions and be more radical in the way they constructed the programme.

Rachel observed this small group beginning to work more effectively together: they became more open and franker with each other. As they got to know each other they became less territorial and more willing to stand in the shoes of potential students and think deliberately about the outcomes they wanted to see from the programme. Rachel was encouraged by the results of this exercise and recognized that key to her own leadership was the need to ensure that the right people were in the room together exercising an appropriate level of freedom in their thinking. Rachel recognized she did not need to be present, but she needed to set a forward-looking, constructive tone so that the conversations between members of different departments were open, forward-looking and not territorial.

As Rachel developed different ways of helping academics work more effectively together she recognized that she needed to apply to herself some of the lessons she was enabling others to learn. Rachel accepted she needed to be less territorial and work jointly and more openly with her fellow deans so that partnership and collaboration were at the centre of the way things were done within the university and not occasional by-products.

As Strategy Director for a charity, Jean's natural inclination was to ensure there was one clear, published, unequivocal strategy. She came from a commercial organization where strategic objectives had been clearly defined, with consistency of message being seen as critical to business success. Jean's natural approach was to want to see uniformity of strategy covering every aspect of the charity's work with a consistent pattern and interpretation in every region. Jean's natural inclination was towards uniformity of approach, but she recognized that the local teams needed to be energized through having a reasonable degree of discretion. If they were just doing what the centre told them to do their commitment and willingness to be innovative would be limited.

Jean recognized that a national strategy needed to include scope for local variation. There needed to be the opportunity for local committees to decide how best to implement the strategy and how to rank priorities so that staff and volunteers were motivated to deliver effectively. Jean became conscious that the manner in which the charity expressed its priorities in a particular region affected the readiness with which funds could be raised within that region.

This insight about this interplay between centre and local groups enabled Jean to become much more flexible in her thinking about the use of freedom when taking forward the strategy. When Jean visited some local areas she was hugely impressed by the energy that existed at this level and recognized that the health and effectiveness of the charity in the future depended on these local people. Hence Jean began to always involve some people from local areas as she developed different aspects of the strategy.

Questions for reflection

1 What might hold you back from enabling others to exercise their freedom?

2 How best do you balance consistency from the centre and freedom which enables people to be at their most energetic and creative?

3 Who might you mentor going forward to enable them to think through the freedoms they have and how they use those freedoms effectively?

4 How regularly do you reduce your freedom to act because you are giving to others the freedom to make decisions?

Section C

Living Out Responsibility

In this section we look at how we can live responsibly within the freedoms we have. We start with seeing responsibility as a joy rather than a burden and then reflect on sitting both seriously and lightly to responsibilities. We reflect on the importance of ensuring sound governance and how best leaders can live with the myriad of expectations placed upon them.

We consider an approach to responsibility involving knowing where your red lines are, bringing pragmatism while recognizing your principles, and avoiding the blame game. We discuss how to keep learning from what goes well or less well and then reflect on balancing responsibilities across the whole of life.

10

See Responsibility as a Joy and not a Burden

When responsibility is thrust upon you, how best do you see it as a joy and not just a burden? There will be moments when responsibility feels like burden, especially at 4 a.m. or when you feel isolated and unsupported. When you are going through a phase when responsibility feels a burden the benefit can be that it forces you to think seriously about the components of your responsibilities and the approach you are going to take to them.

If you feel burdened by responsibility over an extended period then your energy is sapped and potentially your effectiveness reduced. It can then help to describe the nature of the burden you are carrying and talk through how you can reduce its weight or carry it more easily. Might the burden be shared with others or might it be helpful to see yourself carrying this burden for a season rather than it being a near permanent weight on your shoulders?

When you take on responsibility it is worth trying to reflect as clinically as possible on what elements of the responsibility will feel like a burden and how best you will handle those aspects, and seek to ensure that you can contain the size of the burden so that it does not contaminate other areas of your life. Perhaps there is the opportunity when you take on a role to specify what aspects you will not be taking on so that expectations are clear about where you will put your energy and focus.

Is it a contradiction to think of responsibility as a joy? As you take on responsibility it is always worth reflecting on what aspects might provide you with a sense of fulfilment. What doors might responsibility open up in terms of engaging with people, which you find stimulating? What areas of knowledge or insight might you be able to gain because of the new responsibilities?

As you take on any responsibility it is always worth reflecting on what opportunities might flow and how these opportunities could open up new horizons both professionally and personally. I often work with leaders taking on new responsibilities. I encourage them to talk through what they are enjoying most about these responsibilities and what has made them smile. Where has there been an element of fun in building new working relationships?

One newly promoted director talked through with me what had helped him fully engage with his new responsibilities in a way he had found enjoyable. This individual talked of the following elements that helped him live with his new director-level responsibilities:

- Focusing on what makes a difference and what matters most
- Taking seriously the need to develop the strategy
- Keeping people focused on the overriding priorities
- Treating organizational dynamics lightly
- Building mutual support
- Seeing the humorous side of crises
- Allowing senior staff to run their areas
- Recognizing what helps maintain personal resilience.

Also important for this newly promoted director were:

- Not defending things that do not need to be defended
- Not feeling overly responsible for individual items and keeping a sense of overall responsibility for aggregated results
- Avoiding one-upmanship.

Key to this individual seeing responsibility as a joy and not a burden was his thinking through his narrative as a leader at a time of major change. He saw his responsibilities as including equipping the team at all levels, unleashing other people's energy, enabling people to change previous assumptions, bringing bottom-up empowered leadership and applying a strong theme of inclusion. The words around which this director framed his leadership approach were about seeking to innovate, inspire and include, alongside a strong sense of incubating ideas. This individual recognized that what would strengthen his effectiveness as a leader would include seeking to identify the joy and satisfaction in the work he was asking other people to engage with.

Geoff recognized that a lot of the people working in his supermarket came to work for the income and not because they particularly wanted to work in a supermarket. Many of the jobs people did were fairly routine. Geoff recognized what it was like to spend hours stacking shelves or sitting at a terminal as customers paid for their groceries. Geoff was adept at enabling anybody working in the supermarket to feel as if their job was worthwhile. He was always complimenting staff on the quality of the work they were doing. Filling the shelves effectively was just as important for the supermarket's success as recruiting the right people to work in the store. Geoff was relentless in his affirmation of individuals: he was careful to use words that were not platitudes. He spotted the contribution of individual members of staff and complimented them in a very precise way.

Geoff's motive was to reinforce this shared sense of enterprise in which all the supermarket employees were engaged. He brought a sense of fun. Geoff knew who he could tease gently and who needed regular, repeated affirmation. Whenever Geoff's responsibilities were feeling like a burden his antidote was to walk around the store and encourage those who were getting on with their work in a purposeful way. When he saw something that was not going as well as it should be his first inclination was to talk with the relevant team leader rather than intervene directly as he did not want to disrupt lines of responsibility that were working effectively.

Rachel struggled with some of her administrative responsibilities. She would far rather be talking to students or doing her academic research. Planning ahead for the allocation of resources felt like a burden she would prefer not to carry. She had to force herself to think about the benefits that would flow for staff and students as a result of the way resources were allocated. Using resources in a deliberate and forward-looking way would enable some members of staff to take forward projects that would be fulfilling both for them and their students. At the same time Rachel recognized that there would be some unhappy people. Rachel had to hold in her mind the joy of some and the disappointment of others, recognizing that there were going to be winners and losers as a result of inevitably difficult decisions.

Questions for reflection

1 Can you lift a burden off your shoulder and examine it to see why it is causing you angst?

2 What aspects of your responsibilities make you smile? Can you hold onto that perspective even when the burdens seem heavy?

3 What opportunities do your responsibilities open up which enable you to engage with people you find stimulating?

4 How best can you inspire others so that their responsibilities feel more like a joy than a burden?

11

Sit Both Seriously and Lightly to Responsibilities

I have seen some people become so burdened by their responsibilities that they have become a shadow of their former selves. Some of them have become increasingly overweight, or drink in an unhealthy way. Responsibility in these people has created a sense of anxiety with unhelpful physical manifestations. For others the sense of anxiety has led to disturbed sleeping patterns with resulting irritability or limited attention spans. Anxiety can feed on itself and create a situation where leaders become increasingly nervy, unpredictable and edgy with tasks left half done and energy deployed in a seemingly haphazard way.

Sometimes leaders recognize the danger signs and are able to take corrective action. Quite often the weight of responsibilities has created an unpredictability in behaviour which is hard for the individual and others to manage. How can we sit both seriously and lightly to responsibilities in order to minimize the destructive effects of responsibilities getting the better of us? The right response will vary between individuals. Part of the answer for some might be as simple as how they sit. Do we physically sit in a fixated position with our eyes glued on a screen for extended periods? Physically moving and walking around on a regular basis helps loosen us physically and emotionally, enabling us to begin to put individual issues into a wider context.

Physical movement can be helpful in enabling leaders to hold together different responsibilities and not be overwhelmed by them. The physical movement might be a brisk walk, a measured stroll, an intensive run, a timed swim or an extended cycle ride. What matters is choosing a type of physical activity that helps you put responsibilities into a wider context. As you move, the sense of physical movement can enable you to move through an issue you are dealing with, become unstuck and able to identify a potential way forward.

Often in coaching conversations an individual will be talking through how they prioritize different responsibilities and see some of the timescales more clearly. My role as a coach is to ask open-ended questions to enable someone to explore the boundaries of their responsibilities and how those responsibilities can be shaped in new ways. The process of talking through different pressures with a trusted mentor or advisor can result in the individual gaining more clarity without their interlocutor saying much. The process of articulation is helping someone clear their thinking and observe why they are feeling the way they are on particular issues.

Sitting lightly to responsibility is not about abdicating responsibility. There are times when it is helpful to park a responsibility for a season. It may be that you need a break and can return refreshed to that responsibility. It may be that you carry that responsibility for a season as it is not appropriate to pass that responsibility onto someone else until a later time. It could be that you have to say you will cease to continue with a responsibility at a particular future date in order to prompt a conversation about who will succeed you, or whether that particular responsibility is going to be continued to be carried out.

Bob felt he was responsible for everything that happened in the church where he was the minister. He needed to remind himself on a regular basis that he was managing volunteers. Sometimes these volunteers would do tasks to the standard that Bob would apply to himself. In some areas these volunteers would be far more effective than Bob, but volunteers can be unpredictable and sometimes tasks were not done on time or to an appropriate standard. Bob had learnt how to sit lightly to situations where others did not fully carry out the responsibilities they had agreed to. Bob was conscious that he was both the leader and a pastor in relation to volunteers. He could not afford to be overly demanding of his volunteers: he had to accept that there would be a variability in the quality and timeliness of what was done.

Bob recognized that he needed to be serious in the way he shaped job descriptions and talked with individuals and teams about what it would be good to progress. He sought carefully to build teams so that there was a shared responsibility for actions to be completed. He brought a philosophical approach, recognizing that if 60 per cent of the commitments that people had given were delivered, then he should view this as good progress.

Bob recognized that he must not blame himself if some responsibilities were not fully carried out. He needed to accept that a church had chaotic elements because it was a melting pot of people from different backgrounds with different assumptions. He knew he had to celebrate the fact that his congregation included senior executives alongside those who were mentally and emotionally challenged. There were those in his congregation who thought that a church minister could do nothing wrong, while others, he suspected, thought that the church minister could do nothing right. With such a diverse mix of people in the congregation, Bob had conditioned himself to hold lightly to the way certain responsibilities were carried out. Bob was not going to let slip the importance of providing a community space where people could reflect on faith and life and as a consequence not be overwhelmed by their day-to-day responsibilities.

Mary was a very conscientious and thorough civil servant. She prided herself on the quality of her submissions to Ministers. Her reputation had been built on her attention to detail and her ability to anticipate the questions that would be most important to Ministers. Having become a member of the Senior Civil Service, Mary recognized that her role was increasingly one of quality control rather than writing all the submissions herself. She needed to mentor her staff so they understood where Ministers were likely to be coming from and could put proposals forward in a way that carried conviction. She needed to stand back more and let her staff develop the confidence to engage effectively with key people inside and outside the department.

Mary had built a good working relationship with one of the junior Ministers but was deliberate in trying to ensure that those reporting directly to Mary were able to develop a similar quality of relationship with this Minister. On some occasions Mary would decide deliberately not to be available for a particular meeting in order to help build the working relationship between the emerging leaders in her team and the junior Minister. Mary was careful not to abdicate her responsibility: she was readily available if her staff were facing difficulties in engaging with this Minister. Mary talked through with this Minister that it was in the Minister's interest to be able to engage effectively with a number of people and not just her, hence the Minister was fully on board with the approach that Mary was adopting.

Questions for reflection

1 When might you be at risk of bringing an over-serious approach to carrying forward your responsibilities?

2 What would it mean for you to sit more lightly to your responsibilities without abdicating them?

3 What responsibilities would it be timely to pass on to others?

12

Ensure Good Governance

Good governance is essential if organizations and their leaders are going to thrive. It provides an essential framework within which individuals can exercise freedom responsibly. Governance can sound a bureaucratic word limiting freedom and choking responsibility. Good governance is a limiter of individual freedom because it defines responsibility effectively. Any organization needs to have a clear governance structure with clarity about roles and responsibilities. Formalized project management structures can also sound bureaucratic but when they work well, they build in appropriate checks and balances to ensure that each responsibility is set within a wider context of proper oversight and accountability.

For any leader it is important to be clear who they are accountable to and on what timescale. The accountability might be to one person or to a committee. A clear definition of roles and responsibilities enables an individual to know how much freedom they have and what the boundaries are to that freedom and the expectations they are operating within.

Responsibility may well not just be on one person. Within a charity the Board of Trustees and the CEO both carry interdependent responsibility. A UK Government Minister has responsibility to Parliament alongside a responsibility to the Prime Minister. The Permanent Secretary in a government department has responsibility to both the relevant Government Minister, the Head of the Civil Service and to Parliament for the proper use of Government funds. These are complementary rather than contradictory responsibilities.

It can be helpful to draw a distinction between accountability and responsibility. A leader might delegate responsibility for the delivery of particular tasks to one of their staff, but in delegating responsibility they are not reducing their overall accountability for what happens as a result of delegating responsibilities. Where you hold accountability for tasks or areas where you have delegated responsibility it is important to be clear how you will exercise your oversight so that the checks and balances in place are workable. You need to know about progress and barriers with a frequency that gives you proper assurance, while not inhibiting the leadership scope of those people you are delegating responsibilities to.

Shared responsibility can be a key element of good governance. Parents have a shared responsibility for bringing up their children. The Chair and Chief Executive of an organization have a shared responsibility for the health of an organization. Job-share partnerships involve complete interdependency with a shared responsibility for leading the team and effective outcomes. Shared responsibility needs clarity in definition and a strong personal sense of mutual support. Human and organizational factors need to be aligned for partnerships to work well.

Some people saw John in his role as the Hospital Chief Operating Officer as a stickler for detail. He would be insistent that for any task the responsibilities and lines of accountability were clear. He had seen too many cases where a project had started off with a lot of goodwill but an absence of structure had meant that, after a while, the project had fallen into abeyance. John was insistent that before any project was signed off there needed to be clarity about who was leading on which subject, what were the measures of success, the timetable for the delivery of different stages and the review points to assess whether adequate progress was being made.

John was also insistent that the sponsors for any project committed appropriate time to review progress at key intervals. John was as direct with the medical staff as with the administrative staff. Experience had taught him that medics, while being highly disciplined in the operating theatre, could become unpredictable when operating in an administrative sphere. John respected the medics and knew that they could bring a structured and disciplined approach when it was in their interest to do so. John was not going to let the medics treat the project requirements as boring, irrelevant bureaucracy.

Jean, in her leadership role at the charity, was not particularly impressed by the trustees in her first encounters with them. She saw the trustees as guardians of the past, able to talk at great length but limited in their understanding of strategic possibilities going forward. To Jean they often seemed to be focused on one aspect of the work of the charity in which they had invested a lot of time and energy. The trustees wanted to tell her things at great length but did not seem particularly interested in listening. Jean's CEO counselled Jean to be more patient with the trustees. Her CEO recognized the limitations of the trustees but emphasized that they represented the views of members and brought a realism and a pragmatism that could not be ignored.

Jean began to spend more time getting to know some of the trustees and resolved that she would not dismiss them in her own mind as quickly as she had been doing. Jean went on a couple of visits with trustees and was gradually building up respect for their insights. The trustees were not as disciplined in their thinking and approach as Jean had been used to with the senior executives she worked with in previous commercial organizations, but the trustees represented the whole of the charity. She began to appreciate that there are always nuggets of truth in what they were saying, even though these nuggets might be buried in a deluge of words.

Jean enjoyed meeting volunteers working in different parts of the country. They were the lifeblood of the charity. Jean accepted that she needed to keep praising the volunteers for their contribution. She recognized that the volunteers felt they owned the organization even more than did the senior leadership as they had contributed to the charity over many years. For those volunteers over the age of 50, working with the charity was a key part of their lives and kept them alert and fully engaged as citizens. Jean recognized that she had to manage volunteers through influence and suggestion. They were not willing to be subject to precise direction from her and, therefore, the hand of governance needed to be carefully moderated if it was to be effective.

Questions for reflection

1 How might good governance be at the top of the 'to do' list rather than at the bottom of the agenda?

2 What checks and balances need to be part of good governance to enable you and your organization to thrive?

3 How can good governance build a stronger sense of shared ownership and joint enterprise going forward?

13

Live with Expectations

Expectations are an unavoidable fact of life. Having clear, agreed expectations can be hugely positive: the problem comes when expectations become unclear, overbearing and never-ending. Many of our expectations are based around relationships and what we expect of other people – how we expect them to treat us, and what we expect them to do. Unmet expectations lead to disappointment and frustration. We can become upset if others are not delivering what we believe are reasonable expectations.

Those who follow a leader bring expectations about:

- The destination: what it looks like, what can be expected when we get there, what is the recognition when we get there?
- The journey: how long will it take to complete, how hard is it going to be and what is it going to feel like?
- What roles people will take, who is responsible for what, and where does the role of the leader begin and end?

These expectations become focused around the leader. The leader can feel they carry all the responsibility in ensuring these expectations are fulfilled, which can lead to an overwhelming sense of carrying burdens for others.

It is not possible for every leader to know what the journey and the destination is going to look like. Team members will, consciously or unconsciously, have their own expectations about what is going to happen. It is impossible for the leader to foresee and address all these expectations. People's expectations change either because they lose sight of what the leader originally communicated, or their own unrealized expectations surface at some point.

When I begin working with a leader my first questions are about the expectations that others have of them and they have of themselves. Starting with the expectations of your boss helps frame a clear understanding of what your responsibilities are and how much freedom is available to you in order to exercise those responsibilities. Expectations may be at many different levels. They may be about the outcomes, but they can also be about how progress is made, who is consulted and what type of consultation is expected with other key interests. Key is an understanding of the timescale for delivering on expectations. It may be that responsibility for delivering certain outcomes is unambiguous or there might be flexibility or a lack of clarity on timescales. If there are different interpretations of what success is or the timescale for implementation, a lack of trust can easily develop.

Working with individuals in teams in a range of contexts which are fast moving has brought home to me the importance of expectations being clearly defined and understood, with an opportunity for them to be cross-examined against tests of reality.

Sometimes expectations can feel oppressive, but that is the reality in which we have to operate. Parents frequently have expectations about what their children will learn. Shoppers have unrealistic expectations about every product they buy being absolutely perfect. Other unrealistic expectations lead to frustration and sometimes unreasonable behaviour. As a leader we sometimes have to accept that there are people who will enter discussions or negotiations with us with completely unrealistic expectations and then blame us when the answer has to be no.

Bob was conscious that a lot of different groups had expectations of him as a church leader, including church members, the church governing council, assistant pastors, the local community and the wider church authority. Some expected him as a church leader to be focusing on visiting parishioners. Others expected him to be a superb preacher. Others wanted him to be a manager and a fundraiser.

Bob felt the pressure of living in a goldfish bowl with parishioners observing how he chose to spend his time and what he decided to do on holidays. He felt the weight of expectation about how he used his money, his leisure time and his friendships. Bob lived with the complication that he was called both to provide leadership in the church and to pastor his church members. He was conscious that if he disappointed people too much they might reduce their financial giving or go to a different church. Bob did not have a line manager breathing down his neck, but sometimes he would have welcomed the opportunity to talk openly and more frequently about some of the issues he faced with a senior leader within the broader church.

Bob kept reminding himself why he had become a church minister. He had entered a situation where there would be expectations on him which would sometimes be contradictory and often unrealistic. Bob knew that he had to be comfortable in himself about why he continued to be a church minister. He needed to keep a perspective that ensured he did not have an over-developed sense of responsibility. Yes, he was a pastor and responsible for members of his church, but it was for church members to make their own decisions about their own lives and how they spent their time and resources. All Bob could do was set a tone about the relevance and application of Christian understanding.

Bob recognized that he needed to keep a careful eye on how he renewed his energy and resolve and how he kept key relationships healthy and forward-looking. Bob acknowledged that he had more flexibility in the use of his time than did many people and, therefore, spending an hour in a gym in the second half of an afternoon was a practical step he could take that was not available to many other leaders. Bob got used to taking a break in an afternoon as his evening would inevitably include church meetings.

Jean felt a weight of expectation on her as the Strategy Director of the charity. She had taken a significant pay cut to move from a commercial organization to the charity but sensed that other employees at the charity felt she was being generously paid. Jean sometimes felt that the attitude of her colleagues was a punishment to her for earning significant sums at the commercial organization. Because she was relatively well paid at the charity, Jean felt acutely the expectations on her.

In her interview for the post Jean had set out clearly what she would draw from her private sector experience and how she could transform the approach that the organization took in its strategy work. Perhaps Jean had created much stronger expectations than she now felt comfortable with. It had been right to set out a clear way forward in her interview: the upside was that the Chair of the trustees and the CEO knew exactly what they had signed up for when they offered the role to Jean. Now it was for Jean to deliver; sometimes she regretted the persuasive way in which she had set out how she would deliver the next steps on the strategy for the organization.

Jean comforted herself that she would much prefer to be in a job where there were expectations on her than in a role where nobody cared what she did or delivered. At least the fact there were clear expectations on her meant that she knew her role was valued. The expectations also meant that she had leverage when it came to resourcing and to the content of publications by the charity. Jean sometimes felt frustrated by the expectations upon her, but the interest in her area did mean that she was going to be listened to and able to influence.

Questions for reflection

1 How far do you fully understand the expectations upon you?

2 How aligned are the expectations that others have of you and your own personal expectations?

3 How much freedom do the current expectations leave you?

4 What expectations of others or yourself do you need to seek to change?

14

Know Where Your Red Lines Are

How much freedom do you want to have? What is an expectation that you would regard as unreasonable? If you are asked to do something that you feel uncomfortable about, how would you raise your concerns? At what point do you raise a warning sign if you think that actions are being taken that border on the inappropriate?

It is easy to say you would not cross red lines, but it is not always easy to decide what action is appropriate or inappropriate. There are some things that are clear. You may conclude that you are not going to exercise the freedom to break the law, act with impropriety or subvert authority that is properly in place and recognized.

You may have the freedom to modify how your values are applied but you may decide that keeping your values consistent is central to your bringing moral authority. As soon as you are seen to be devious and disingenuous, those around you will consider these to be valid behaviours.

As a leader you may feel you have a considerable degree of freedom. You may be under a lot of pressure to deliver on certain outcomes and recognize there are different ways of delivering those outcomes, some of which are consistent with the organization's values and acknowledged behaviours, while others might be beyond what is deemed normally acceptable. What is key is to be honest with yourself about when you are applying your freedoms in an entirely responsible way that is within the accepted norms of the organization and the culture, and when you might be choosing to take responsibility for actions that some would regard as underhand or disreputable.

Sometimes politicians set red lines which are in contradiction with each other. The risk is one red line is set because of an appeal to one constituency and a different red line is set in an appeal to a different constituency.

Living out responsible leadership involves setting assumptions or red lines that are compatible with each other so that your approach is seen to have integrity. It also means being consistent in the application of your assumptions, so you are seen to have personal integrity. Oscillating between different red lines or being unpredictable in how you apply your red lines means that respect for your decision-making can rapidly become questioned.

John, as Chief Operating Officer, was often frustrated that he was expected to be the conscience of the hospital. Lots of managers in the hospital wanted to flex the way money was spent or resources allocated. They sought to view decisions about the use of resources as suggestions. A lot of managers in the hospital seemed to have no scruples about seeking to get their own way. From their perspective it was always in a good cause – that of enhancing patient care. John could become irritated when he saw that the pleading to protect the quality of care in one part of the hospital was inevitably going to have a detrimental effect on the availability of resources in other parts of the hospital.

John accepted that encouraging budget holders to act responsibly required that there was both specificity about how resources were to be spent and a degree of freedom so that budget holders could use their resources as effectively as possible. At the same time as recognizing the importance of giving budget holders discretion, John knew that he had to be utterly insistent in saying 'no' when individuals wanted to stretch the boundaries in an unacceptable way.

Mary had been trained by an experienced civil servant who was relentless in sticking to the evidence. This colleague was perfectly happy to say to a Government Minister that the evidence did not justify statements they wanted to make.

Mary had been schooled in the belief that it was right for a civil servant to speak truth to power and to be willing to be unequivocal in the advice they gave. Mary had then become wary when she had observed how one Minister became so fixed on a particular point of view that she refused to hear or read any evidence that suggested her viewpoint was speculative rather than authoritative.

Mary recognized that statistical data could be interpreted in a variety of different ways. When new data became available, she wanted to be satisfied that she understood the implications of the data before it was presented to Ministers. Mary had developed a slight fixation that her Minister would inevitably want to interpret the figures in a particular way that would be slightly dubious. Mary had learnt that she needed to talk through new data carefully with Ministers and talk about different possible interpretations. She recognized the pressures on a Minister to bring good news. She also recognized that if a Minister stretched the facts too far this would rapidly be exposed in debate in the House of Commons.

When Mary said to the Minister that a particular statement the Minister wanted to make would be inconsistent with the evidence she expected a stony silence or a dismissive smile. Slightly to her surprise the Minister began to talk through a different way of formulating how the data might be viewed. In dialogue over the next few minutes they began to formulate a way of expressing the figures that Mary thought consistent with the evidence and the Minister thought was positive enough to be supporting points the Minister wanted to make.

When the Minister wanted Mary to prepare a letter that was very critical of the Opposition's policies she knew she had to treat the request with care. It was one thing to provide facts about the consequences of the policy proposals put forward by a range of different people, including members of the opposition. It was reasonable to draw attention to some of the consequences of such policies, but Mary did not see it as her place to be drafting emotive sentences for the Minister to sign about the policy proposals from the Opposition. Sometimes it felt as if Mary had a difficult path to tread between support for Ministers and maintaining her integrity as a civil servant who was focused on the evidence. It helped that there were always people she could talk to within her department to enable her to think through what she said to the Minister and her next steps.

Questions for reflection

1 To what extent are your assumptions and red lines based on thoughtful consideration of issues or purely on inherited norms or prejudices?

2 How best do you ensure that some of your assumptions and red lines are not in contradiction with one another?

3 How best do you handle a situation where your assumptions and red lines are being heavily questioned by others?

4 Who can you most readily talk to about the red lines you are needing to address?

15

Bring Pragmatism, While Recognizing Your Principles

In some people's minds, describing an individual as pragmatic raises questions about their values, whereas for other people, to be described as pragmatic is a mark of admiration. One person's pragmatism is another person's lack of principle.

To be described as dominated by principles can either be a mark of respect for an individual's integrity, or an implied criticism that they are rigid and inflexible. Being a responsible leader is often about bringing pragmatism while recognizing key principles. Sometimes balancing principle and pragmatism is a practical way forward and leads to finding the lowest common denominator approach. Sometimes principle is paramount. Legislative requirements and financial rules or regulations are tampered with at your peril. Where an organization's stated values and behaviours are ignored the culture can easily become tarnished and an organization's reputation eroded. If there are abuses of power and authority that mean individuals are not treated fairly or consistently then stated principles become meaningless.

Pragmatism is not the instant use of freedom in response to emotional reactions. Pragmatism is about handling situations wisely where there are conflicting principles. It might involve reaching a negotiated outcome where different principles have been held in balance.

We may want the ideal outcome, but sometimes 'the best can be the enemy of the good' and an approach needs to be taken which is pragmatic while ensuring that key principles are not compromised.

Being pragmatic involves recognizing that our human nature includes a flexibility that means we are not always consistent or true to the principles we articulate. Being willing to be pragmatic allows creative dialogue to take place, enabling new approaches to be developed in handling longstanding issues.

Pragmatism can be about avoidance. The individual with an alcohol problem will do all they can to hide their addiction in a work context. They can become experts in deceit in order to hide their problem, with long-term consequences for the quality of the work they do. The individual for whom the bonus is a significant driver may use their freedom to manipulate figures in order to get the best possible financial outcome, thereby misusing the financial responsibility they have been given.

Sometimes being pragmatic is an important quality. The negotiator involved in settling a big contract will be applying certain principles, but also knows that at a certain point they will need to be pragmatic about what deal is delivered.

It is worth reflecting on what the principled use of pragmatism is in your context. Pragmatism that is principled is based on reasoning, shared decision-making, open and honest communication, and clear reviews of potential outcomes. A leader needs the freedom to be pragmatic combined with a sense of responsibility only to use pragmatism after careful consideration of the evidence and after dialogue with interested parties.

When pragmatism is being applied it is always helpful to have an independent person who can be a sounding board about propriety and reputation. Sometimes it is valuable to talk to a relevant regulator or auditor prior to a decision being made; they will not be able to approve your decision but they can throw light on how such a decision is likely to be viewed and assessed.

It can be revealing to reflect on how you have sought to balance principle and pragmatism in the past. In what circumstances has it been helpful to focus on principle rather than pragmatism? What have you learnt from situations when you have been purely pragmatic and the outcome was not as constructive as you had hoped?

Sometimes ways of making decisions and the behaviours in organizations have become frozen in time. Ways in which decisions are taken become regarded as principles when in fact they are only a description of how things have traditionally been done within that organization. Sometimes it is right to exert a degree of freedom in looking again at procedures that have become regarded as principles. There may be a need to break through previous conventions and build new procedures that are applicable in the current context: pragmatism is then important in recasting a set of processes which are based around up-to-date, pertinent principles.

Rachel, as a university dean, was often appalled that academics who believed in clarity of evidence in their academic work seemed to regard evidence as irrelevant when it came to decisions within the University. In her experience academics frequently had misconceived notions about what their role was in ensuring successful outcomes. If numbers on a course were falling the problem from the academics' perspective was often about the marketing and not about the construction of the course. Rachel recognized that she had to be relentless in pushing the academics to revise outdated assumptions and look at the evidence afresh about student expectations.

Rachel felt that her decisions were being questioned persistently by the academics. They kept producing anecdotes which they presented as contradicting the approach Rachel was advocating. It was exhausting working with academics who acted like a 'dog with a bone'. Rachel learnt that when it came to decisions about future courses she had to be clear on the key principles that needed to be applied: they needed to be simple and unambiguous to prevent them being interpreted in a myriad of different ways.

Rachel recognized that she had to be pragmatic in the

decisions she made in order to keep the academics motivated, but it still meant disagreeing with their preferred options on numerous occasions. Rachel knew she had to hold her ground when some of the academics were relentless in seeking to reopen decisions. She knew that if she reopened decisions too often this would fuel their relentlessness. Rachel resolved to always consider the concerns of the academics, but once a decision was made and her key arguments set, to then regard the issue as closed for the coming year.

Geoff, as a supermarket manager, felt that some of the decisions made by head office on products were random. He recognized that there was no point in a constant barrage of e-mails questioning judgements made by head office. Geoff had to choose his moment to express concerns. An issue needed to be significant for him to invest time in putting evidence together to question the appropriateness of a decision.

Geoff knew that the best way of influencing head office was to be part of early decision-making about future product and marketing policies. Complaining after the event frequently had little impact. Feeding in ideas at a formative stage was much more likely to be successful. Geoff knew that some of the buyers in head office were more willing to be influenced than others. He chose the people he spoke to and the issues that he raised. He knew that the most effective approach was to talk about pragmatic decisions by customers rather than questioning whether certain principles were being effectively followed and developed.

Where Geoff was firm on principles was about behaviours within the supermarket. Rudeness and discourtesy were dealt with immediately. One of Geoff's key principles was that staff and customers should always be treated with respect and courtesy even when they were being questioned about theft. Sticking to key principles about the way people are treated was both an expression of the values of the company and of Geoff's personal values. He was also pragmatic because he knew that a calm and purposeful staff was a consequence of consistent, respectful behaviours, however difficult the issues that were being dealt with.

Questions for reflection

1 When can principle and pragmatism be at odds with each other for you as a leader?

2 When should principle trump pragmatism?

3 When should pragmatism trump principle?

4 How best do you assess whether you are balancing principle and pragmatism effectively?

5 When might you be in danger of applying pragmatism in a way that borders on the irresponsible?

16

Avoid the Blame Game

There are always reasons why we are facing adversity and it's often possible to identify someone else who can be blamed. But blaming somebody else does not get us nearer to a way forward and a solution. Blame is a rampant epidemic in politics across the western world. There was a time when blame was attached to the policies of political parties that took a different view to your own. Currently it seems just as fashionable to blame people within your own political party as well as blaming people in other political groupings.

We may be amused when the injured toddler blames the table for getting in the way or being in the wrong place. A key part of parenthood is enabling youngsters both to take responsibility for their actions and not to resort to blaming others or even blaming inanimate objects for their disappointments.

When a pupil does not perform as well as their parents had hoped there is a tendency among parents to blame the teacher, the school, the curriculum, the Government or anybody else who can in some way be said to be accountable for their child's education. A doting parent can be fixated on others having caused problems rather than accepting that their parenting might have been flawed and the youngster might be struggling to find their place in the way the classroom operates.

An equal risk is to keep blaming ourselves for everything that goes wrong. The parent who blames themselves for every small blemish in the behaviour of their child is likely to become inward looking and depressed, losing the spontaneity and joyfulness needed to keep children cheerful.

In a work context we can face risks both of blaming others for our problems or blaming ourselves for anything that does not go quite as well as we would have hoped. Blaming others can mean we do not face up to our part in creating difficulties for ourselves. Blaming ourselves can mean we get stuck in remorse and are unable to move forward in a fresh and constructive way.

When we are inclined to blame others it is worth being systematic in thinking about what the causes of the problems were and why people reacted in the way they did. Recognizing the nature of the pressures others have been addressing helps us understand why they took the decisions they did. If we are intent on blaming someone else we can be blinding ourselves to any understanding of their reasoning, however flawed it might be. When our inclination is to blame ourselves it is worth thinking through how others would view the situation and to what extent they would see our decisions as key or whether they see us as one of a number of contributors to a situation.

Bob learnt that there were mutterings from older members of the congregation that younger people were not involved in church life. These mutterings implied that Bob, as the church leader, had not devoted enough energy to the young people and, therefore, it was his fault that the number of youngsters had declined. Bob felt this criticism personally, which made him both frustrated and sad. This was a responsibility that was not purely on Bob's shoulders, although it felt as if it was a burden that he was carrying alone.

Bob put engagement with young people on to the church council agenda and encouraged an open discussion. He steered the discussion towards what the church as a whole was going to do to seek to engage more with its young people. Bob was clear that he wanted to build a shared sense of ownership for next steps with responsibility being delegated to a group of which he was a member rather than the chair.

At the same time, Bob decided to have a discussion with some of the people whose views had been reported to him. In open discussion with Bob these individuals were clear that they were not blaming Bob: they were genuinely concerned about this issue and a number volunteered to contribute to funding for a youth worker. Bob was glad that he had tackled this issue as soon as he heard that there was a perception that he was being blamed for the limited youth activities. As a result of tackling it directly and addressing it in the key church council meeting, clearer plans were put together with a financial commitment supporting a strategy for this age group.

Mary had worked closely with a Government Minister who had been reshuffled elsewhere. The new Minister had a tendency to blame others for the problems they inherited and was surprisingly critical of her predecessor, as well as being dismissive about what officials had contributed to her areas of policy over the last decade. Mary felt that the new Minister was blaming her predecessor unreasonably, which made Mary feel uncomfortable in her working relationship with the new Minister. Mary did not think it would be diplomatic to raise this issue directly with the new Minister, but she brought a wariness in her engagement with her. She thought it important to ensure that she had a clear audit trail of approvals for decisions made by the Minister.

Mary recognized there was a risk that the new Minister might be positive to her face and critical about her behind her back. Mary decided she needed to build up some immunity to potentially duplicitous behaviour and recognized that she needed to keep her distance and not get too close to the Minister. At the same time she knew she had to build a rapport with the Minister so that the Minister would trust her judgement and her commitment to take forward what the Minister expected.

Questions for reflection

1 How best do you handle your own tendency to blame other people for your misfortunes?

2 How best do you stop yourself blaming others or yourself unreasonably when things go wrong?

3 How best do you address an insidious blame culture when it is at risk of becoming prevalent in your organization?

17

Keep Learning from What Goes Well or Less Well

I have known individuals who are always offering to take on greater responsibility and have thrived with additional responsibility, but then something goes wrong under their watch and their confidence is shaken. Their track record of success has meant that they are not used to setbacks. For those who have been used to events unfolding in their favour a major setback can be very unsettling and destabilizing. My perspective in coaching, however, is that we learn far more from our failures than our successes.

In competitive sports an individual or team is continually having to take responsibility for choosing a strategy where often the strategy is not successful. Repeatedly pushing an attack in a particular way which is always repulsed may increase the stamina of a sportsperson, but may also have limited chances of success. A good sportsperson repeatedly changes their approach and takes full responsibility for their actions. They learn about themselves and the opposition every time they make a move. They have to take responsibility for the shots or moves that go wrong while celebrating the approaches that prove successful. Through their training, they take the responsibility for keeping refining their approach and reactions so that the likelihood of success increases.

An individual sportsman or sportswoman may be in a competition where they are acting alone, but they will always be supported by a team who are dedicated to enabling the individual to act at their best in a competitive situation.

When a support team is working well every member has clear responsibilities to contribute to the success of the sportsperson. If the individual is not as successful as they had hoped there is potential learning for each member of the support team. A poor result either leads to dejection or to an acknowledgement that adaptions are needed to increase the likelihood of a better outcome.

A different risk is that when there is a good outcome the opportunity to maximize the learning from that situation is lost. There can be a complacency when something goes well which leads to an absence of reflection about what success teaches. Bringing an acute sense of responsibility to fine-tune the learning from successive events is key to the long-term sustainability of any venture. Teams in competitive cycling have benefited from an incremental approach to developing the learning from what has gone well. A relentless focus on continuous improvement has enabled many successful organizations to thrive even more.

What is key to maximizing learning from what has gone well or less well is a strong sense of individual and shared responsibility to spend time reflecting on what has been learnt and building that into next steps. Time that is set aside for review and crystallizing of learning is never wasted. The risk is the tendency to move on to the next project rather than fully assimilating the learning.

Geoff had the discretion as the supermarket manager to support local charities. When he looked back he recognized that he had chosen to fund some ventures purely because of the persuasive nature of their advocacy. He recognized that he needed clearer evidence about the credibility and capability of a charitable venture before he chose to support it. He accepted that there was a conundrum whereby he wanted to support some new initiatives where there was a limited previous track record of success. Geoff was willing to take responsibility to back innovative ventures. He wanted to ensure a reasonable feedback loop without this being too bureaucratic.

Geoff wanted to support charities that his staff were engaged with. He saw this as good for both staff morale and staff development. The views of staff provided quality input when deciding which ventures to fund. He wanted staff members who were part of a charitable activity to play a responsible role in contributing to that charity's endeavour. Geoff had the discretion to give some paid days off to staff involved in significant, local charitable activities. Geoff invited staff members who were engaged in charitable activities as part of their work time to be clear what they had learnt from their engagement with the charity and in particular what they had learnt from activities that had gone less well than they had hoped.

John sometimes felt that he had been browbeaten into making decisions at the hospital. Evidence had been presented to him that on the face of it was significant, but with the benefit of hindsight the evidence was less robust than it should have been. John was adept at asking probing questions so that those putting forward new initiatives were clear how they were going to be evaluated. John was equally persistent in setting expectations about the learning that flowed from initiatives that had not worked as well as had been hoped. John had the potential lever that those who resisted his requests for evaluation might, in due course, be seeking further resources from him. Therefore, John knew that his requests that outcomes were reviewed carefully would not be ignored.

John was very conscious that if something went wrong in the hospital few people would be lining up to accept responsibility. The phrase 'success has many parents while failure is an orphan' rang true for John. He observed a limited willingness for managers to take responsibility for actions that had not worked out as successfully as they had originally hoped. John would ask each of his direct reports once a month to share an example of something that had gone wrong under their watch and what they had learnt from that situation that they were going to apply going forward. If someone was minded to say to

John that nothing had gone wrong on their watch, John would look disbelievingly at them and ask them to reconsider. He took the view that if nothing had gone wrong on someone's watch they were not being ambitious enough in taking forward their responsibility to develop the effectiveness of the hospital.

Questions for reflection

1 To what extent is it your natural reaction to take responsibility for something that has gone wrong?

2 What approaches work best in your experience to ensure proper considered reflection by individuals or groups about the learning from what has gone wrong?

3 How best do you ensure that you maximize your learning from when you had taken on responsibilities that have worked out well or less well?

18

Balance Responsibilities Across the Whole of Life

All leaders go through phases when they feel that work is dominating their lives. That is fine for a period but if it is unrelenting for long periods judgements can become distorted. There is clear learning from the emergency services which put limits on the time that any individual can operate on frontline activity. An engineer leading a major project knows that they must not become over-dependent on a very limited number of people: there needs to be a group of experts who can be used interchangeably to ensure the smooth running of an enterprise if there is relentless pressure over an extended period.

When you are in a role which is relentless for a period of time, it may not be realistic for you to take on significant responsibilities in a charitable or local organization. But taking on responsibilities outside your main sphere can add hugely to your understanding of organizational dynamics and how different organizations deal with priorities and ambiguity. When someone is taking on new responsibilities in a work context I often ask them if they are developing a new interest or taking up new responsibilities outside their primary work area. It can provide a helpful antidote to ensure that the day job responsibilities do not become overwhelming if an individual is developing an interest or taking on some responsibilities in another sphere.

I have often encouraged emerging leaders in busy organizations to consider whether they might become a charity trustee or a school governor in order to learn about handling responsibilities in different types of organizations. I suggest they are realistic about the time commitment that they are taking on, while at the same time inviting them to sit different responsibilities alongside each other so that they are able to see what is working in different contexts and continue to develop insights into what ensures effective leadership.

A key question for many emerging leaders is how they balance family responsibilities for ageing parents and young children as well as work responsibilities. This is increasingly pertinent where both parents are in demanding roles. There are an increasing number of examples of partners weighing up their relative responsibilities at work and the extent to which one parent might deliberately take on fewer work responsibilities for a period. Juggling responsibilities effectively depends on the quality of communication between partners and their willingness to put their personal ambition on hold for a period when opportunities for advancement, personal fulfilment or learning might be greater for their partner.

I have known individuals who for a period have not sought enhanced leadership responsibilities while at the same time taking full responsibility for developing their personal learning. They have been building their portfolio in the way they influence and engage with other people in order to develop their long-term credentials. They are taking full responsibility for their career development and recognizing that their long-term development is more important than short-term progress.

Rachel felt that she had a long list of responsibilities as an academic dean. Rachel also had two lively children and was committed in a lay leadership role at her church. All three responsibilities were important to her. At the very centre of her life were her two children: her responsibilities to them came before anything else, but she had decided that she needed to earn an income so that the two children had a secure home life. Rachel led a team at church that was responsible for the church fabric, which was also important to her. Rachel recognized that her key responsibility at church was steering her committee, which included a number of retired people who had the time and energy to take forward particular projects. Rachel's experience with this church team was helping her develop a leadership approach of steering rather than rowing. Motivating volunteers was reinforcing in her skills that were important in motivating people within the university.

Rachel's family and church commitments meant that there were times when she had to leave university at a particular time in the late afternoon. These external responsibilities forced Rachel into a discipline of using her time at work in as effective a way as possible. Rachel recognized she did not always get this balance right and could sometimes feel over-responsible for small decisions within the university. She was glad that she was engaged in other spheres which helped her keep her perspective when it came to making a decision about whether to stay at the university for another hour or leave promptly at 6 p.m.

Jean's mother was terminally ill. Jean felt a strong sense of responsibility to care for her mother and felt guilty when she put work first. Sometimes her mother would telephone Jean at work and Jean would either be brief on the telephone or sometimes ignore the calls. Jean felt she was becoming increasingly hard-hearted towards her mother. She had a couple of friends with whom she could discuss how she best engaged and cared for her mother.

Jean needed to make decisions on behalf of her mother: it was key that Jean spent quality time with her one remaining parent. Jean recognized that she had to hold in balance the responsibility to her mother and her responsibility to the charity which had employed her as Strategy Director. These responsibilities were not in contradiction with one another but sometimes it meant that there were difficult decisions to be made about how she used her time. Sometimes she felt she did not make the best decisions about priorities and often questioned her own judgements, but Jean recognized that she was the only person who could make decisions about how to split her time between her responsibilities as a daughter and her work responsibilities. She did not want to take advantage of the goodwill of the charity as she recognized that donors had given generously to the charity. On the other hand she felt a debt of loyalty to her mother who had been consistent in her care and support over the years for Jean.

Questions for reflection

1 What are your guidelines in how you balance different responsibilities across your life?

2 How might responsibilities in one area of life inform your approach to responsibilities in another area of life?

3 How best do you deal with particular challenges about potential conflicts in the split of your time between different responsibilities?

Section D

Balancing Freedom and Responsibility

Balancing freedom and responsibility is a never-ending process. The right balance for one season in life may need to be overtaken by a sequence that is more relevant for the next phase of life. In this section we look at finding an evolving equilibrium going forward and then look at exploring different work patterns. We address looking after your wellbeing and then redefining what success looks like. The section concludes with reflecting on responsible engagement and communication, while still keeping an overall approach that is forward-looking.

19

Find an Evolving Personal Equilibrium Going Forward

How we balance different responsibilities will evolve over time. Whatever pattern works for us now is unlikely to be optimal in a year or two's time. We can be so pleased that we have found an equilibrium that works for us that we stick rigidly to it and are not as flexible as perhaps a new context might warrant. We can become comfortable in a routine that has served us well in the past and seek to avoid the frictional cost of changes in our routine.

I have observed couples who find it difficult to find a new equilibrium when they first have children. Sleep patterns are disrupted and the baby does not respond to being treated as a project. Over time parents learn the art of having a plan A for when the child is awake, a plan B for when the child is asleep, and a plan C for when the child cannot decide whether to be awake or asleep.

For many parents responsibilities for young children disrupt their personal equilibrium and their effectiveness at work is diminished for a period. They become focused on the short term and less able to address strategic issues. On the other hand the responsibilities of parenthood can create a much stronger resolve about discipline in the use of time. I have seen parenthood resulting in time being used much more deliberately with a resulting increase in effectiveness in meetings. The parent who knows they have to leave work promptly at 5 p.m. can either become over-anxious and too wrapped up in the detail, or more focused in ensuring that tasks are done and contributions made in a deliberate and timely way.

Family circumstances can often create the need and the opportunity to change how different responsibilities are balanced. With ageing parents there are practical and emotional pressures that can be unpredictable. When children leave home there is a renewed freedom alongside some loss of a sense of purpose. Children leaving home can coincide with their parents' retirement or semi-retirement, providing a combination of reasons to find a new personal equilibrium. Even more acute can be the time when someone retires from paid employment and needs to reflect fundamentally on how to use their time and energies going forward. Uncertainty at this stage in life can create a loss of confidence and reduce the feeling of self-worth. For some the phase after taking retirement is an exciting period of finding a new equilibrium. For others this phase can result in turning inwards and becoming a shade grumpy and narrow-minded.

The relevance of such stories is that there will be times when changes in life circumstances mean that the way freedom and responsibility is balanced needs to change. These periods can be seen as unsettling and destructive of what has been good in the past. They can also be seen as an opportunity to reshape activities in a way that provides a new phase of personal fulfilment and satisfaction.

In the first five years of his ministry leading the church, Bob put a lot of emphasis on developing younger leaders. He mentored individuals and encouraged their participation in leadership programmes. He began to see the results of these efforts towards the end of the five years. Inevitably, a couple of people in whom he had invested time moved geographically elsewhere. Bob was initially disappointed by their decisions but recognized that his mentoring of them had led to a new-found confidence within them which enabled them to take on these new responsibilities elsewhere.

As Bob moved into his second five-year period at the church he passed leadership in particular areas to some of these emerging leaders. The consequence was that Bob had more time to give to some ecumenical activities. He also took the opportunity to do an MBA at a local business school, which he found stimulating as it meant he was engaged with leaders in different spheres. Bob recognized that some people in the church would feel that he was less available than he had been in the past. Bob was deliberate in explaining why he was passing responsibilities to some emerging leaders and the benefits for the church of his doing wider ecumenical activities and further leadership development.

Bob was aware that in his first five years leading the church there were times when he did not disengage on his days off or ensure he took retreats when he could reflect on his journey and next steps. Bob was clear that he needed to ensure that on his days off he was not available and was not dwelling on his church leadership responsibilities on these sacrosanct days. He put in the diary a three-day retreat every six months which he knew would provide a valuable opportunity to take stock of how he was balancing his different responsibilities.

When Rachel felt weighed down by her responsibilities at the university she took comfort in the fact that leadership roles in universities were often exercised for a time-limited period. As dean of the department she could, after five years in the role, say that she wanted to be focused in her next phase on her academic work rather than leading a department. She was deliberate in not using the phrase 'going back to academia' as that would appear to her and others like a retrograde step. Rachel had observed other colleagues move into a further phase of research leadership after a period of administrative leadership. Knowing that this opportunity would be available to her in a few years' time enabled Rachel to handle her current responsibilities with a greater personal acceptance. Rachel deliberately kept in touch with her academic interests and went selectively to key conferences, developing thoughts about what academic priorities she wanted to focus on in due course.

Questions for reflection

1 Does your personal equilibrium need to evolve because of the changing pattern in your responsibilities?

2 For how long do you think your current way of balancing your responsibilities is going to work effectively?

3 What changes in the pattern of your responsibilities do you want to address going forward?

4 What opportunities are you looking forward to which might open up to you as a consequence of some current responsibilities diminishing?

20

Explore Different Working Patterns

As a child born in the first half of the twentieth century, I grew up with the assumption that work patterns would normally be a nine-hour working day for five and a half days a week. When working in busy jobs within Government in the 1980s and 1990s the working day was more like ten to twelve hours a day for five or more days a week. For people in demanding roles in the 2020s, the consequence of electronic communication is the pressure to be available 24 hours a day for seven days a week. The consequence of this expectation about availability has been growing signs of stress and anxiety in a significant number of people, alongside a much more deliberate acceptance of the need to box time for work and to legitimize different working patterns.

Employers are increasingly recognizing that there is a benefit for them in encouraging more flexible working practices. It enables them to attract and retain the best talent. A growing number of individuals are prepared to trade off some loss of income to make space for other commitments, while still wanting to contribute in challenging roles. Part-time working, nine-day fortnights and compressed hours are already available in many organizations. Technology allows far more people to work from home for part of their working time.

The growth in job-sharing has reinforced the concept of flexible working patterns and provides something extra to the employer, as a job-sharing partnership may bring a set of skills, styles, perspectives and experience which is unlikely to be found in one person. Job-sharers tend to be highly motivated and determined to show that two heads can be better than one.

Job-sharing offers talented people the incentive to stay in an organization and enables them to develop their capabilities and advance their careers.

This can be contrasted to some part-time roles which can be seen by their occupants as leaving them on the sidelines marking time. For some people, however, part-time roles with specific responsibilities are exactly the right way forward, both for them and the organization they are working for.

Successful job-sharers coach and learn from each other. This mutual mentoring can reduce the demand on their manager to be a sounding board and can provide support in times of stress, for example, when dealing with poor performance or an unexpected crisis.

Job-sharers talk about the personal benefit of having shared responsibility. They always have in their head the voice of the other person. They find that responsibility can sit more lightly when they are in a job-share partnership that is working well. On the days when they are not working they can focus on other commitments without feeling an overriding sense of responsibility to keep in touch with what is happening at work. They would be acting irresponsibly in relation to their job-share partner if they engaged with work activities when their job-share partner was on duty.

Those in job-share partnerships recognize that there are risks they need to be mindful of. They need to build in the freedom to be frank with each other about what is working well or less well. They need to be open about when they feel frustrated with each other and when expectations might be diverging. They know that they have to be deliberate in the way they act jointly in managing their staff so that there are not inconsistencies in the way they are living out their responsibilities.

A major change in work patterns in recent years has been the growth in virtual working. Many organizations are not providing desk space for all their employees and regard hot-desking as the most efficient use of space. Other organizations are relying increasingly on virtual communication. The coaching organization which I helped found, Praesta Partners, started off with each coach having an individual coaching room. We moved to shared access to coaching rooms, and then to having just a back office and then to becoming a virtual organization. The clients noticed little difference in the nature of the coaching other than, for some of them, a change in the locations for the conversations.

The consequence of greater flexibility in where people work has increased the expectation of personal responsibility in the way time is used. There are many examples of how it has resulted in leaders using time much more effectively, but it does require a rigorous discipline in what tasks are done where and how communication is taken forward so that people within an organization feel fully engaged with their colleagues.

Mary had considered the possibility of working in a job-share. She had not previously thought that this was the right approach for her but she was deliberate in being supportive of job-sharers within her organization and had recently appointed a job-share partnership in a key role. She recognized the extra transactional costs that resulted from having a job-share partnership in the team but the benefits far outweighed these transactional costs. She had appointed a job-share partnership where the two people brought complementary skills and were energetic throughout the time they were in the office. There was no tailing off in productivity on Friday afternoon.

Mary experimented with different working patterns. She booked into the diary working from home every alternate Friday, which provided valuable opportunities to catch up with e-mails and to have one-to-one phone meetings with staff members. Mary recognized that she did her most constructive longer-term thinking in the morning, hence once a week she would allocate two hours for longer-term thinking early in the day. Her secretary was under clear instructions not to put meetings in her diary in this two-hour slot. Mary would either work at home, or in a coffee shop near the office, or in a space within the office well away from where she would normally sit. Creating this private space for a reasonable length of time each week proved productive for Mary.

There were times when Mary recognized there was resulting frustration for others because she was not available, but if Mary had been at a meeting she would not have been free to engage with her colleagues. Mary thought one of the great benefits of flexible working patterns was the flexibility it gave her and her staff, provided she was deliberate in using this freedom in a responsible way and communicating clearly how and why she was using the time.

John was initially sceptical about flexible working for staff in the hospital and got irritated when people were not available. The hospital had to run 24 hours a day: he believed that he had to be available to deliver the work whenever it was needed. This philosophy meant that John was relentless in his time commitment to work. He was often in the hospital for 11 hours a day and always accessible at the weekend. This approach meant that people relied on him more and more and kept putting further responsibilities on his shoulders. The risk was that John could at times feel exhausted. On his days off he would sometimes sleep for much of the day. His family life had taken a battering because of his commitment to work and his marriage had ended. It felt to many people that he was married to his work. John enjoyed carrying the ultimate responsibility for the wellbeing of the hospital and used the freedom he had in the use of his time to be utterly committed to the hospital.

John's colleagues felt that John was putting too much pressure on both himself and other people through the way he exercised his responsibilities in a relentless way. The medical director took John out for a coffee and had an open conversation with him about the effect that John's relentlessness was having on his colleagues. He was making them feel inferior and unmotivated as a consequence of his excessive work commitment. The medical director suggested to John that he should make some adjustments in his working pattern in order to look after his wellbeing, and signal that it was his choice to work such long hours and it was not John's expectations that everyone else did the same.

John recognized that he needed to shift his approach and attitude. John decided to take a three-week holiday and began to put careful thought into how he was going to use this time to follow up personal interests. John began to make it more explicit that it was his choice to work the hours he did and that he was a strong supporter of flexible working patterns when people were balancing personal and work responsibilities. What mattered to John was that he recognized and openly said to others that it was his choice to work the way he did and that he was not expecting others to work in the same way.

Questions for reflection

1 What is your ideal working pattern that will enable you to fulfil your responsibilities to best effect?

2 How much freedom do you have to vary your work pattern in a way that enables you to fulfil your different responsibilities?

3 What might your next steps be in shaping the way you adapt how you apply your time and energy in fulfilling your responsibilities?

21

Look After Your Wellbeing

I have known people who have been working so hard that they have forgotten what they have done the previous day. For one individual it was an indicator that he had been overstretching himself when he received a telephone call about an e-mail which he had no recollection of sending. It is a wake-up call when you are reminded of something that you have no recollection of having done.

Taking responsibility for your own wellbeing involves recognizing when you have been working with such intensity that your brain is not able to catch up with what you are driving it to do. Taking responsibility for your own wellbeing includes being as objective as possible about your levels of personal resilience and what can enhance or diminish that resilience. It involves recognizing when uncertainty can create a sense of threat. It can include training your brain to focus on priorities by scheduling blocks of time for different types of work and modes of thinking. It involves being conscious about how your brain works and how you can work with the grain of your preferences. It might involve practising noticing your emotions as they arise in order to get better at recognizing their presence earlier. It can involve accepting that, when you are experiencing a strong emotion, it might be necessary to move into a different physical space so that you can put this strong emotional reaction into perspective and not be overwhelmed or blinded by it.

Creating 'shafts of stillness' has proved for many people to be an effective way of moderating their energies and keeping events in perspective. Turning your brain off for five or ten minutes might initially seem an indulgent luxury, but can often prove to be re-energizing and revitalizing. Creating 'shafts of stillness' might involve cultivating stillness as an attitude of mind, allowing yourself to cherish good moments, creating personal space where you are uncluttered, and developing the ability to block out or tolerate external noise. Shafts of stillness can include allowing silence in conversation and not always rushing to fill the space. It can include using stillness to calm yourself down and move yourself into a different frame of mind.

Looking after your wellbeing involves being deliberate in recognizing the freedoms you have and don't have and then seeking to build in rhythms that work for you that are consistent with your wider responsibilities. It involves recognizing when you are best equipped to solve difficult problems, and watching the consequences of trying to do too many things at once. Key is recognizing what can distract you and what the rhythms are that help you feel more in control of your own situation and your creativity. There are moments when looking after your wellbeing requires you to be ruthless in your time and energy and alert to when you might go into a downward spiral, alongside the need to be deliberate in taking corrective action.

Looking after yourself involves taking responsibility for your physical, emotional, intellectual and spiritual wellbeing. These areas may well overlap. Being engaged in team activities can reinforce both physical and emotional wellbeing. Engaging in dialogue with interesting people can reinforce both intellectual and spiritual wellbeing. Intellectual wellbeing benefits from being engaged in a range of different activities and not just your primary work activity. Being engaged with people in areas of common interest where there is a strong sense of vocation can help both your emotional and spiritual wellbeing.

What is key is not letting your wellbeing spiral out of control. There may be elements of your personal circumstances that are exhausting where you feel in danger of being overwhelmed. What matters is the extent to which you are able to stand back from the mix of emotional pressures and seek to be deliberate in the steps you take to keep your physical, emotional, intellectual and spiritual wellbeing in reasonable equilibrium.

Geoff knew that he got edgy if he sat down for too long. He had to keep physically moving around, hence walking around the supermarket twice a day gave him relevant data for his leadership role and gave him the physical exercise he needed to keep calm. Geoff's main hobby was the triathlon. He found the swimming relaxed him, and the cycling helped build a rhythm in both his body movements and in his thinking. The running was purely an exercise of persistence and stamina which gave him a lot of both personal grief and satisfaction.

Geoff thought that one day he would compete in an Ironman triathlon, which includes running a marathon, but not yet. Geoff was conscious that he should not be dominated in his thinking by the economics of store management. He enjoyed reading novels provided he was alert enough to read the text and not fall asleep. Keeping up the rhythm of reading a novel every month kept Geoff's brain alert. Doing sudoku felt futile in one sense but gave him satisfaction and a sense of achievement.

Jean recognized that she was at risk of falling into anxiety and depression sometimes. After the initial elation of being released from the commercial environment in which she had worked, she went through a period when the lack of progress in her work meant she felt down and at risk of having low periods.

Jean recognized that there was a pattern whereby she could become over-anxious and not able to think clearly about forthcoming decisions. Jean had learnt she had to accept that she would sometimes go into a phase where she was not operating as effectively as she would at her best. When in those moods Jean knew that it was best not to seek to make key decisions. She needed to park certain decisions until she was in a clearer frame of mind. She recognized that talking to some trusted individuals would help her move through a period of depression. Jean had to hold on and wait until the depression lifted. Jean was disappointed that the shift in role had not eradicated these low periods.

Jean had to accept that there was a pattern in her depression that she was stuck with which was unlikely to change radically. She used approaches that helped ameliorate the consequences and knew who to talk to in order to help put her moods into a different place. Jean recognized that it was important not to take on excessive levels of responsibility in her strategy role as having tasks which she felt she could not fulfil would increase the risk of depression. Jean knew she had to be structured in accepting and carrying out her responsibilities and in the expectations which she allowed others to have of her. Jean recognized that one of the advantages of being in a senior role was that she did have the freedom about how to use her time. This flexibility helped shape the way she carried forward responsibilities in a way which worked with the phases of her depression.

Questions for reflection

1 How much do you consider that looking after your wellbeing in a deliberate way is your responsibility?

2 What freedoms could you use more effectively to build rhythms in your use of time and energy that will work well for you?

3 What are the danger signs that you can be alert to when you know you will be at risk of not maintaining your wellbeing as responsibly as you should?

22

Redefine What Success Looks Like

When I write a book I am continually redefining what success looks like. It is useful to have a benchmark figure about the number of chapters I seek to draft in a day as it helps structure the day, but inevitably there will be events that mean the expected number of chapters to be written needs to be reduced, or occasionally increased if the flow of thought and words is good. When the words are not flowing it is helpful to move to a completely different activity and let the brain process subconsciously the themes that will flow into the next phase of writing. Success is then redefined as greater clarity about the themes to be explored in a chapter rather than the number of words committed to the page.

When looking after grandchildren success may be an outing where the children are cheerful and engaged. Success at mealtimes with young children might be about keeping reasonable order without too many disagreements. At the end of the day success is happy, tired children going to bed peacefully and sleeping soundly. Looking after grandchildren is a reminder of how measures of success keep changing depending on their moods, the weather and what happens to be catching their imagination on a particular day.

If we have set a very clear aspiration about delivering on a particular objective and the progress has been limited we can exhaust ourselves worrying about what has caused the delay. There are moments when we need to accept that the original timescale is not going to work and that the measure of success needs to be amended. The scientist who completes an experiment that does not lead to a fruitful conclusion may describe the experiment as a failure; or they could describe it as successful because it has demonstrated that a particular approach is not going to lead to a breakthrough. When something goes wrong it is helpful to acknowledge to yourself that this is a successful outcome in that you have learnt that a different approach is needed for the future.

Each of us will have different approaches to motivating ourselves. Some of us need clear targets with measures of success acting as a fundamental part of how we focus our energy and time. For others measures of success are destructive and undermine the effective use of time and energy. What is important is that our colleagues understand what enables us to be at our best and how different definitions of success affect our motivation and our effectiveness. Parents recognize that too much pressure on the successful development of certain skills in children is often counterproductive. A happy child is more willing to learn and explore new ideas than a child who feels driven into submission to achieve specific goals.

When someone is continually overstretching themselves by relentlessly pursuing targets they can be overstretching their capabilities in a way which is counterproductive. We have perhaps a responsibility to our colleagues to help them have a clear understanding about what realistic success is and a recognition about how best to respond when success is not easy to come by.

Mary had seen success as a perfect working relationship with the Government Minister to whom she was responsible. She increasingly accepted that there would be ups and downs in such relationships. Success was not about perfection. It was about an equilibrium which allowed constructive dialogue to take place, recognizing that relationships would not always be straightforward. Success was not about a relationship with no disagreement. It was about how differences could be handled in a way that allowed the Minister to be honest in their concerns and Mary to be frank in her observations. Success was about getting to a way forward recognizing that interchanges could sometimes be messy and include tangential elements.

Rachel had hoped to write four academic papers each year and became increasingly frustrated when this did not prove possible. She recognized that she needed to revise her aspirations by halving the number of academic papers she planned to write and set aside some time during the summer to do the research to enable papers to be written. Rachel set out with the intention of having a mentoring conversation with each of her direct reports once a fortnight. She soon recognized that this approach was not necessarily welcomed, nor was it realistic. She revised this to having review conversations once a month with a time limit of one hour for each conversation. This more realistic perspective was accepted as an appropriate sequencing. Rachel fully accepted that her initial intent was not viable or the best use of her time and that of her colleagues.

Bob had set as a measure of success an increase in the numbers present at church services. He had introduced an evening service for younger people which had worked well with good attendance, but when a cohort of youngsters went off to university numbers dropped. Bob needed to ensure he did not regard this drop as a failure. It was a natural consequence of a particular year group leaving. What he wanted to do now was invest in another generation while recognizing that it would take time to build up their interest and commitment.

Bob recognized that a significant proportion of people only came to church once or twice a month. The pattern of coming every week was now less often the norm for young families. Retired people also seemed to be more active than in the previous generations and would often be away and, therefore, not involved in church every week. Bob recalibrated the way he measured participation in the church away from purely weekly Sunday church attendance to the number of people involved in some way in church life. What he discovered was that, while numbers at Sunday services had been reducing, the numbers involved in different aspects of church life had been growing. This reinforced for Bob the importance of using success measures that were apposite in the current context.

Questions for reflection

1 To what extent does your definition of success need to be revised?

2 When you revise your measures of success how best do you do it in a way which motivates you for the future rather than creates a sense of disappointment and failure?

3 How best do you take responsibility for things that have not been successful when you recognize that some of your actions were misplaced?

23

Practise Responsible Engagement and Communication

Where a team has worked hard on a project and reached a conclusion, there is always the risk of the team thinking their job is done, when their job has only just begun. Writing a report is the end of the beginning, not the conclusion of the project. If any project is going to have an impact much depends on the way it is communicated and whether different interests are engaged effectively in turning debate into outcomes that are delivered.

Thinking responsibly about engagement is not about persuading others to your point of view. It is about seeking to build a shared understanding and an agreed way forward wherever that is possible. Where agreement is going to be difficult, responsible engagement is not about ignoring other parties and pretending that they are going to disappear. Responsible engagement with those with whom we disagree is about maintaining courtesies in human engagement and setting out clearly and calmly the reasoning that has led to particular conclusions.

Communication that is founded purely on your preferred approach irrespective of the facts is the height of irresponsibility. Assuming that the louder you shout, the more valuable your perspective is unlikely to lead to an outcome where there is a strong sense of shared endeavour and an agreed way forward.

Responsible engagement involves identifying all of those with an interest and seeking to understand their perspectives and speaking into their situations as openly and cogently as possible. When I led on various consultations for the UK

Government I always sought in the final results to point to the influence that each organization we had consulted had had on the final outcomes. When people recognize that they have been heard and acknowledged in some way they are much more likely to acquiesce in the way forward, even if they might not agree fully with each aspect of the conclusions.

Responsible communication is about facts being expressed clearly and unambiguously, with a clarity about reasons for decisions and their implications. Turning speculative assumptions into irrefutable facts is at best speculative and at worst irresponsible. Too often advocates of particular ways forward oversell the merits of their favoured approach in a way that others eventually see as questionable, and can represent figures to support their approach in a way that is disreputable. Figures that are flaky have too often been sold as absolute truth. The views of some individuals have too often been represented as the views of a majority. At least the epidemic of fake news has meant there is a much greater wariness about how figures are deployed, but too many of us find ourselves influenced by the selective use of statistics and the views of those who bring an emotive and blinkered view about next steps.

John was having to deal with emotive pleas from medical and nursing staff on a never-ending basis. Disaster was always described as imminent if John did not act quickly. He was used to either being shouted at or receiving abrupt e-mails that implied he was indolent. However irritated he became as a result of the emotive way in which some staff tried to influence him, John sought to keep his cool and keep a focus on evidence. When a decision needed to be made John sought to be painstaking in consulting people, recognizing that he would often receive a dismissive and unhelpful response.

John thought carefully about how decisions were to be communicated, always seeking to give reasons for decisions and to set out key figures. John sometimes felt that his communications were either ignored or immediately dismissed, but quiet voices in the organization would tell him that setting out the arguments clearly, both orally and in writing, was always helpful in enabling people to understand why decisions had been made. John recognized that often there was not the time for effective communication but he tried, as far as possible, to talk to key people when decisions were made which were not likely to be warmly received, or at least to send a personal message which expressed understanding of their concerns.

Geoff often felt he was caught in a situation where communication was one way: from the head office to the supermarket branches. Geoff thought about how best he communicated upwards in ways that would be received as constructive feedback. He frequently wanted to write a cross e-mail. He would draft such an e-mail and then in most cases decide not to send it. However, the process of drafting the e-mail helped Geoff clarify his thinking about implications and next steps.

Geoff recognized that if he wanted to influence key people in head office it was best to start by commending these people on the work they were doing and recognizing where good progress had been made. He would then identify two or three points where changes needed to be made and was clear in setting out the benefits that would flow from these changes. Being selective and focused in his communication with head office was the only way he could readily influence them. Geoff knew that if he showed irritation with head office he would be branded as purely interested in his supermarket. He had to demonstrate that he was making a contribution that would affect the effectiveness, reputation and profitability of the whole enterprise.

Jean was conscious that the charity depended on a wide range of different donors. Corporate donors needed to be handled in a very different way to individual contributors. As Strategy Director, Jean recognized that she needed the good will of donors. She committed time to talking with some of the bigger corporate donors in industry to understand why it was in their commercial interest to support the charity. She recognized that the corporate donors were not donating out of the goodness of their hearts alone, while still recognizing that there was a strong philanthropic emphasis in some commercial organizations.

Jean was at pains to seek to understand why individual donors supported the charity and why individual volunteers gave a considerable amount of time to help with the work of the charity. Jean enjoyed this dialogue with donors and volunteers and recognized the importance of keeping up high-quality engagement. Sometimes it was the communicating and engaging with the trustees that gave her more angst than engaging with donors and volunteers. She felt the trustees wanted to tell her what to do, whereas the funders and the volunteers wanted to hear from Jean what she was seeking to do. The learning for Jean was to consider carefully why different groups behaved in the way they did and how best to engage and communicate to develop a stronger sense of shared purpose and joint responsibility going forward.

Questions for reflection

1 When does responsible engagement become irresponsible badgering?

2 How best do you ensure that you have genuine two-way conversations and don't just indulge in telling people what you want them to believe?

3 How best do you commit enough time to being engaging and communicating in a way that is fair to the evidence and respects the perspectives that a range of different people bring?

Section E

Next Steps

The final section of the book encourages you to reflect on your next steps as you take your leadership contribution to the next level. It encourages you to keep growing in self-awareness, to recognize your voice and influence, to shape teams that work for you and to develop the next generation. It addresses building a sustained legacy and bringing an openness of mind to whatever might come next for you.

I encourage you to look at the themes in this final section with a sense of future possibility as your work and life circumstances evolve, and as your own priorities and preferences go through different phases.

24

Grow in Self-awareness

We are on a never-ending journey of learning about ourselves, the contexts we are in and the potential impact we can have. When we view ourselves as fully competent in a situation we are at risk of closing the door on further learning. Our insight into what works and does not work will keep changing if we allow ourselves to bring fresh approaches and refuse to be constrained by previous mindsets and a prior understanding of ourselves and the people around us.

We may think that we are completely clear in our understanding of a situation and in our communication with others, but we might be deluding ourselves and not fully recognize how we come over to others and when we are at our most or least influential.

Our self-awareness grows as we push the boundaries of our freedom and keep recalibrating what is working or not working. Our learning is maximized when we take on new responsibilities with an open mind and recognize what we can do well and where we need to further develop our perspective and approach. Our self-awareness can benefit from doing psychometric assessments, listening to feedback from others, listening to our own emotions and experimenting with different approaches.

The most acute growth in our self-awareness can come from our reactions to mistakes made by ourselves or others. We can notice a grumpiness in ourselves that can be more readily transmitted than we might wish to admit. There are points when we need to stand back and reflect what we learn about ourselves from apparent misjudgements and not let setbacks derail us or send us backwards. The best of learning frequently flows from continually pushing boundaries and keeping recognizing the incremental learning that we are gaining.

Mary recognized that she could be reluctant in some circumstances to express her views. The self-awareness that she did not always say what needed to be said prompted her to keep thinking through what the holder of her post should be saying and then saying it. This proved a good way of emboldening her to speak truth when it needed to be said.

John was aware that a lack of patience could sometimes be evident in his approach. He needed good colleagues to tell him when he was becoming too demanding in his tone and needed to become more measured. John could normally recognize when his impatience was beginning to show but welcomed feedback from trusted colleagues at the point they saw the risk of counterproductive impatience showing.

Bob became increasingly self-aware that too much was resting on his shoulders. He enjoyed taking responsibility for developing different initiatives at the church but increasingly recognized that this was not in his best interest or the long-term interest of developing leaders within the church. He recognized he needed to become more self-aware about when he needed to stand back and ask questions and make suggestions rather than taking the lead himself.

Rachel recognized that frustration could sometimes be seen written all over her face. There was a risk that frustration came over as annoying and overbearing to others. Rachel recognized that she needed to be more self-aware about when frustration was at risk of showing. In many ways frustration was a very powerful aid to her understanding of situations and people: it forced her into action, but frustration could also get in the way and be destructive of her good intent. For Rachel, increased awareness about the risks of her being frustrated enabled her to be more deliberate in how she motivated those around her.

Geoff knew he could go into overdrive and come over as

frenetic. His bursts of freneticism could be effective in energizing those around him, but his freneticism could also be exhausting to everyone. The key learning point for Geoff was about pacing his energy and being aware of when it could inspire others and when it could erode their sense of independence and personal endeavour.

Jean knew that she did not handle disappointment well. She needed to prepare herself for when things did not go her way. Jean recognized that she needed to be kind to herself and not push herself too hard or else her emotional energy might collapse for a period. Jean was not inclined to be open with her colleagues about the personal volatility that she could experience. She knew that she had to manage it herself and recognize symptoms at an early stage.

For all these individuals there was a need to be mindful of their continuous learning about their own preferences and foibles and how best they kept up their personal development as leaders. Under pressure they could all revert to a previous version of themselves. In their better moments they recognized that as a result of their leadership journeys they had become increasingly able to use the freedom they had to best effect and exercise their responsibilities in an influential and sustained way. They recognized that it would often be 'three steps forward and two steps back'. They needed to live with their own humanity with its joys and frustrations.

Questions for reflection

1 How would you sum up your growth in self-awareness over the last year?

2 What is the area of self-awareness you are currently focusing on?

3 How best can you use the freedoms available to you to develop your self-awareness further?

4 What will enable you to further develop your self-awareness as you take on new responsibilities?

25

Recognize Your Voice and Influence

Leaders often have more influence than they realize. They may think that progress is slow and that nobody is taking them seriously. They may feel that everything they say is cross-examined in a sceptical way.

Sometimes they might be tempted to express their views more forcibly because they sense that they are receiving a critical hearing. The truth is that their views are being considered, with furrowed brows usually a sign that views are being taken seriously rather than being dismissed. Overstating a case might be counterproductive because it then becomes easier for someone to argue against it. Making your case in a clear, factual, measured way might in the long run build greater credibility and mean that over time your perspectives are more influential than you might realize.

Often the most influential people in meetings are not those who talk the most or the loudest. Influence comes through choosing the right moment and being focused in your contribution. It might be a key question or a pertinent summary, or the reinforcement of a particularly apposite point. It might be the use of a key piece of evidence which helps convince colleagues about a way forward.

When you feel a sense of responsibility to influence next steps, or you feel an expectation from others that you push a point strongly, the risk is that you overstate the case and do not choose the most opportune moment to make your intervention. The danger is that you are more concerned with being able to report to your boss that you made his point forcibly rather than focusing on the outcomes that most need to be delivered.

It is worth reflecting on the nature of the freedom you have to express a view and influence. It might be that you have a designated role in presenting information or a proposal. It might be that you are the guardian of particular interests such as resources, propriety or employment relations. The scope for you to contribute might be as a result of your previous experience of similar activities. It is worth being clear what, in other people's eyes, gives you the freedom to express opinions, and what the nature of the responsibility is that gives you distinctive authority.

When you are hesitant about what the appropriate nature of your contribution is, it can be helpful to think about what type of contribution that the person in your role should be making. Depersonalizing the way you decide about what influence is needed through focusing on what the responsibility of the jobholder is can enable you to overcome inhibitions about making your points. Influencing projects effectively involves recognizing that you have a voice and the importance of being deliberate in how you make your points. When points are made in a domineering or aggressive way they can be brushed aside. If they are made too quietly they can easily be ignored. Using the right tone of voice to make your interventions is key to people wanting to listen to you and being willing to engage with you in a way that leads to forward movement rather than in barricades being erected.

Mary could sometimes feel overawed by some of the senior civil servants she worked for. They could come over as macho and be preoccupied with football or cricket. When one meeting of directors started off with a conversation about football she thought about making the point that the topic was not inclusive as not everyone was interested in football. Mary could feel excluded when her colleagues talked confidently about how they had handled similar situations and current issues. Mary knew from private conversations with some of them that their level of confidence was not as high as their bravado suggested.

Mary recognized that sometimes she needed to let 'the boys' have their say first and then she could make salient points clearly and directly. She was skilled at summarizing progress made in discussions and flagging up consequences. Mary recognized that the best way for her to influence proceedings was to choose her moment to bring her incisive thinking to bear. It did feel like an uphill battle sometimes when 'the boys' appeared to be more interested in joking with each other than listening to her, but she was persistent in the contributions she made. At the end of the performance year Mary was struck by the feedback from her peers who were all extremely positive about her contribution. This feedback gave Mary huge encouragement that her approach was effective.

Bob recognized that he had a more obvious way of influencing people in the church than did most leaders. Each Sunday Bob had the opportunity either to preach at the church or contribute in leading services and flagging up future events. He had the opportunity to engage directly with church members. He saw this as a privilege as he recognized that many leaders did not often have that opportunity to talk directly to their staff or customers in the way Bob did. Bob recognized that this privilege of addressing members of the church regularly came with responsibilities. If he tried to lecture, chastise or cajole those attending church services he was likely to have limited success, with church members deciding to be less committed, to move elsewhere or leave the church.

Bob knew that he had to catch the imagination of those at church services and take them with him on a forward-looking journey. Bob needed to speak in a deliberate, measured way that demonstrated he understood the issues and the questions faced by members of the congregation. Bob recognized he had a responsibility to help church members think about their own lives and opportunities in a constructive way. He wanted to create a context where those hearing his sermons would be invited to think in a deliberate and challenging way about the forthcoming weeks and how they engaged with others in a supportive way in the spheres in which they lived.

Bob did not believe that preaching sermons focused solely on challenge and little on compassion would enable members of the church to play a constructive and influential role in their daily lives. Bob saw his role as encouraging and not criticizing. His was a message of hope and reconciliation rather than failure and judgement.

Questions for reflection

1 When have you observed your contributions being influential beyond your expectations?

2 What is the nature of responsibility on you to be increasingly influential and use your voice in more overt ways?

3 What inhibitions might get in the way of you using your voice and influence to full effect?

26

Shape Teams that Work for You

Expectations on leadership teams in all sectors and countries are heavier than ever. There are stakeholders and regulators to be satisfied, reputations to be protected and finances to be watched. The pace of events is such that there is a constant pressure to make rapid judgements and deliver at speed. There is a premium on a team's ability to handle rapid change effectively.

When Hilary Douglas and I wrote the Praesta Insight booklet entitled *The Resilient Team*, we identified ten key characteristics of teams that stay resilient, namely that they:

- Know what the team is for, and what can only be done by the team acting together
- Balance planning the longer term and dealing with the here and now
- Work together to turn plans into reality
- Are proactive in response to a changing environment
- Pay attention to values and behaviours
- Engage effectively with stakeholders
- Build capability for sustainable change in the organization
- Understand and apply effective governance
- Maintain momentum as team members change, and
- Look after their own wellbeing.

As a team leader you need to balance building a strong sense of cohesion and shared responsibility with freedom for individuals to use their initiative acting as a representative of a team in a range of different contexts. Your responsibility when shaping a team includes allowing team members to work out the best way to work together with their colleagues. You want the criteria for success for the team to be clear and for the team to have worked out how it is going to maintain its focus and resilience in tough times. Ways of doing this can include reminding the team what it is there to deliver (the performance lens) and assessing how well the team understands how it can work together effectively (the resilience lens).

What can be effective is initially helping to shape a team and then allowing the team to run itself. You may indicate that you are going to be involved for a couple of months but then withdraw to let the team you have shaped take responsibility for next steps. You do not want your presence to dilute either their freedom to operate or their responsibility to work together effectively. Shaping teams that work for you might be about setting key parameters and then enabling others to take the lead, with you providing gentle steers and prompts at key moments. Steering a team well can start with your reflecting on what it is only you can do to enable a team to be fully effective. Your personal contribution might be about setting objectives, making appointments, opening up contacts and ensuring there is effective quality control and periodic reviews.

Having set a team off in a particular direction you may choose to limit your involvement to key strategic moments. This is not abdicating responsibility: it is focusing in a clear way on the distinctive contribution you can bring while creating a context whereby team members assume full responsibility for next steps and are uninhibited about taking them forward. Leadership to the limits with teams can be about holding back on your presumptions so that progress is not limited by team members' perceptions of what you would find acceptable.

Shaping teams that work for you might involve being clear what some of the key risks are that could get in the way of the team being fully effective. Resilient teams find ways of balancing planning the longer term with the here and now: recognizing that when a team is dealing with a myriad of issues it can sometimes be overwhelmed by the immediate and ignore the longer term. Perhaps your contribution to a team might be a periodic reminder that the team has responsibility to deliver on the longer term as well as delivering immediate actions.

Because of his wide experience, John had a tendency to think that he could do a job better than others in the hospital. He had a gut reaction that it would take longer to explain to somebody else what was needed than it would for him to do a task himself. He was continually fighting against this inner assumption that no one could do something as effectively as he could. John recognized that one of the ways he could reduce the pressures he felt at work was to commit more energy to shaping the teams that worked for him as, in the long run, this approach would make better use of his time. John invested in team-building activities with his direct reports so that his people better understood each other's experience and preferences.

John made clear that on some subjects he would become less involved. If he was asked a question about what was happening in particular areas, he promised himself, and his team members, that he would redirect that request to the appropriate team member and not seek to sort out the issue himself. John recognized that some people might think that he was ducking his responsibilities if he did not deal directly with tricky requests, but John knew that he had to limit his involvement in order to enable his team to take full responsibility. Too often things would get delegated to him. He wanted to ensure there was a change in practice so that this tendency was significantly reduced.

Jean was used to working with younger executives in her previous role in the commercial world who were happy to push boundaries and take initiatives. She was surprised that a number of people working in the charity were reluctant to take on responsibility or try new approaches. Perhaps because they were being paid less than they might have been in other sectors they did not think they needed to work as hard. Some individuals within the organization gave the impression that they were doing the organization a favour by turning up. Team meetings tended to be fairly flat and uninspiring with individuals seemingly reluctant to express a view or take responsibility for next steps.

Jean was increasingly concerned that progress in a number of areas would be slow unless members of her team upped their game. Jean worked with people right across the organization but did not observe much energy being focused on key forward issues. Jean was frank with her team, asking them what was getting in the way of them being at their best. Jean was able to tease out inhibitions about why they were not contributing more. She realized that some of their contributions in the past had been ignored. Some of her staff had put a lid on what they would willingly contribute. Jean saw her role as encouraging these individuals to open up and to suggest next steps. Some of the staff warmed to Jean's approach. Others felt she was expecting too much of them and were reluctant to take on a greater degree of responsibility, pointing out the number of things that they were already responsible for.

Questions for reflection

1 To what extent are the teams you engage with using their freedoms to best effect?

2 What responsibilities do you have to enable teams you lead or are part of to be effective?

3 In what ways can you steer the teams you are involved in and ensure that your contribution is focused on what only you can do?

27

Develop the Next Generation

Leaders in their twenties and thirties are bringing very different approaches compared with earlier generations. They are more adept at using information technology. They often build relationships more quickly and are more willing to be more flexible in the way next steps are done. On the other hand they can be less loyal to organizations, more short term in their aspirations and less willing to concentrate on the same activities for an extended period. Their willingness to stick at responsibilities over a long period may be less in evidence than for some previous generations.

Developing the next generation is key to any organization's success. Organizations have to be flexible enough to respond to the desire for more flexible working, more immediacy of feedback, more discretion in how tasks are approached and a focus on learning generic skills rather than specific skills related to a particular job.

Building the next generation of leaders includes giving people responsibility early and letting them learn from mistakes. It involves being willing to set aside preconceived notions about the right way of doing things and allowing a more flexible way of turning ideas into practice, while ensuring good governance is maintained.

An approach that has worked well in developing the confidence and effectiveness of the next generation of leaders is a focus on the four Vs of leadership: vision, values, value-added and vitality. This enables emerging leaders to:

- focus on their personal vision about the leader they seek to be in the future

- be explicit in defining and living their values and reassessing life priorities against those values
- be clearer about their value-added contributions and
- be more deliberate in their use of energy, spending quality time on activities that are most important to them, thereby raising and sustaining their vitality.

Core to applying the four Vs is an individual using the freedoms they have to best effect, and bringing a deliberate approach to living out their responsibilities in order to have a value-added impact, and to nurture and develop their vitality. These are aspects of their leadership that cannot be subcontracted to someone else.

Rachel was impressed by the credentials of many of the younger academics in the university. There was a rigorous approach to addressing academic issues and a desire to work in partnership with colleagues on funding proposals. Focusing on analysing individual issues did mean that many of these younger academics were focused in narrow areas and were not always adept at seeing the wider implications of what they were researching.

There was a tendency among these young academics to view their areas of research as paramount and to see the way the university organized itself as something to criticize rather than to be engaged with. Rachel knew from her own experiences that cynicism about organizations was destructive for both individuals and the university. Rachel wanted to inspire some of these younger academics to recognize that influencing the way a university operated was part of the contribution they could make. She suggested areas where some of these young academics could be part of forward-looking planning for the university. Sometimes she had to persuade them quite forcibly but was then pleasantly surprised by the feedback that involvement in wider activities had been stimulating and helped them understand some of the broader context in which they were operating.

Rachel prompted them to think about the type of value-added impact they could bring into these wider conversations. She encouraged them to think through their vision of the type of contribution they would like to be making in five years' time and what sort of university department culture they would hope to be part of.

Rachel recognized that these younger academics were energized by their academic work: she was encouraging them to draw their energy and vitality from a wider range of activities within the university context. They were driven by particular values that were important to them in the subject matter with which they were dealing. Rachel encouraged them to be pragmatic in seeing how their values were relevant to the contributions they could make to a wider range of aspects of the workings of the university.

Drawing from a wider family context, Geoff was conscious that it could be very difficult for ex-offenders to establish themselves in employment. Geoff chose to become part of a scheme of employing ex-offenders and assisting their rehabilitation into a working environment. Geoff did this with sensitivity and never drew attention to what he was doing. He was inspired by some well-publicized examples in other parts of the retail and warehousing sectors. Geoff knew that the arrangements had to be made carefully in order to protect people from themselves in the early stages. He recognized that some of the skills that had led people into activities that had resulted in a judicial sentence could also be used effectively in a work environment. Geoff wanted to catch the imagination of those coming out of a prison environment to recognize that they had personal skills and determination which could enable them to make a success of employment.

Geoff felt it was just as important to inspire those who had made mistakes in their lives leading to jail sentences as it was to inspire reticent employees who had never previously thought that they could take on management responsibility. Geoff recognized that he needed to use a variety of approaches to bring out the best in different people. What was central to the way he sought to do this was to affirm individuals in specific ways when they were demonstrating the potential to look ahead and making good decisions about priorities and people.

Questions for reflection

1 What opportunities are there for you to develop the next generation?

2 Who might others dismiss or ignore who you think it worthwhile investing in?

3 What is the value-added contribution you could enable people to develop whom you work alongside?

28

Build a Sustained Legacy

You have pushed the boundaries and built sustainable new ways of working. As a result, your people are much more flexible in the way they engage with each other. They are less hierarchical and more willing to debate possibilities and are less reliant on the views of one single leader. You have helped develop adaptability in the team you are working with. You have created a 'new normal' in the way people are open with each other and address evidence in thoughtful and open-minded ways. Gone are the silos and presumptions of the past.

There is a risk that you want the new normal to be the perfect end-state which will, like the Roman Empire, last a thousand years. Yet you may well have set off an approach of questioning and looking forward which means that ways of working will continue to evolve.

The way electronic communication is continually adapted, with people getting used to different ways of communicating with each other, means that organizations cannot stand still. They need to build on best practice and respond to the way others are engaging with them.

Sustainability is not about one formula that is going to be repeated a thousand times. Sustainability flows from a mindset of continuous improvement and a readiness to engage with changing evidence, hopes and expectations.

When you move on from a particular area of activity, your sustainable legacy is about the skills you have helped develop alongside the frame of mind you have encouraged. Your legacy might be an open and responsive engagement with changing circumstances that is rooted in a set of values about how people are treated, which leads to a capacity to respond to buffeting and an ability to adapt to new opportunities.

Bob was conscious that he could well be in a leadership role at his current church for a further five years. He was posing the question to himself about whether the legacy of these five years might be a physical legacy of adaptions to the church premises, or whether he wanted his legacy to be more about the engagement of church members within both the community and their work context. Bob was conscious that Jesus had sent out the disciples in twos to engage with the communities around them: much of Jesus' ministry was equipping his disciples to have the confidence to engage with individuals and communities and become influential in the wider world.

Bob recognized that a building project and a focus on leadership development were both compatible with the needs and opportunities in the church community. He needed to make a decision about where he placed his energy. He did not want to rule out the development of some physical space within the church but was clear that this was not where he felt called to use his energy and leadership. The outcome was that a non-stipendiary minister with the relevant skills took the lead on the building project, which was exactly the right way to take this project forward. Bob felt his calling for the next phase was to work with individuals who had leadership roles in the secular world and enable them to become increasingly effective at bringing a Christian influence into decision-making in a range of different spheres.

John wanted to help ensure that the hospital would continue to be focused both on the effective use of resources and on creating an environment where people wanted to work and where patients felt welcomed. As Chief Operating Officer he recognized that any successor would want to inherit a well-run hospital where each aspect of the hospital functioned effectively, but for John this was not sufficient. He was determined that his legacy would be a forward-looking, adaptable workforce who were willing to see opportunities rather than barriers when they looked ahead.

John recognized that sometimes his day-to-day demeanour was not entirely consistent with the attitude of mind he wanted to engender within the hospital, hence he had to keep checking himself when he was at risk of becoming grumpy and defeatist. When he had low moments he had to withdraw briefly and decide what his demeanour was going to be in order to keep developing this forward-looking, encouraging approach.

Rachel recognized that sustainability had to combine a rigorous focus on performance and outcomes, alongside an inspiring and motivational approach to people which brought out the best in them. Sustainability required cheerfulness and positivity and it also required a determination to keep standards high and to be focused on ensuring that data on progress was explicit and not suppressed. Sustainability only happens if there is clarity about facts and an openness to scrutiny. Facts needed to be looked at in an honest, constructive and forward-looking way.

Sometimes Rachel was criticized for apparently being contradictory, that is, very straight and hard on data while very encouraging and personable in development conversations. Rachel sought to be meticulous in explaining why both these elements were important and were reconcilable. It is essential for any leader to combine honesty and clarity about evidence alongside openness and a sense of hopefulness which inspires.

Questions for reflection

1 What do you hope will have been sustained five years after you move on from your current role?

2 What in your context is it most important to sustain to ensure the health and effectiveness of the organization of which you are part?

3 What attitudes are you developing in people which are key to the long-term sustainability of what you are seeking to build?

4 What would you like to be remembered for five years after you move on from your current role?

5 What might get in the way of your building a sustainable perspective on the future among your colleagues?

29

Bring an Openness to Whatever Comes Next

When I am coaching someone approaching the age of 50, I encourage them to think that they could well have 25 or more years ahead of them doing interesting and influential activities. I have seen too many people dream of slowing down in retirement and then become inward-looking in their focus. My task as a coach with people of any age is to encourage them to think forward and reflect on how their experiences and insights can be valuable to other people in the next phases of life.

When I was approaching the age of 55 my eldest son challenged me to reflect on the question, 'If I was 21 again what would I like to be doing next?' This prompt helped me think open-mindedly about the possibility of moving into executive coaching. When I reached the age of 60 my son again challenged me to think on the sixties as the 'golden years' when I would have the opportunity to be engaged in a range of activities without some of the day-to-day parenting and responsibilities associated with early stages of life.

When I reached the age of 70, my younger son encouraged me to enter the next few years with the mindset that there was a further active working phase ahead of me. These three conversations were influential in helping to reinforce an openness to whatever came next. As I write this chapter I am suffering from a minor fracture in my left forearm, which reminds me that whatever comes next might be painful and not always joyful. On the other hand, it reinforces the importance of being open to what might be positive consequences of whatever comes our way. At least the fracture is in my left arm and does not, therefore, disrupt my writing.

On a recent walk with my younger son he challenged me with the question, 'If I was bold what would I do next?' When I gave a fairly modest answer to this question he turned the screw and asked, 'If I was more radical what would I do next?' When we reach particular milestones we want to enjoy the feeling of success or fulfilment that the milestone brings, and also have an eye to the type of opportunities that we might take forward. Reaching milestones might be the moment to push the boundaries and not let our self-limiting beliefs or previous experience get in the way of bold or radical next steps.

There are moments in life when we can be bold or radical because we have more freedom or independence than we had in the past. Maybe we have been inspired in particular ways by individuals we respect. Maybe we are gripped by an opportunity that presents itself. Maybe we see a need for a contribution that we are equipped to make. Perhaps we are frustrated by our own reluctance to take a next step in terms of responsibility and reach a point of being frank with ourselves that now is the moment to make a stand or embark on a new adventure.

Now might be the moment to move from an executive to a non-executive-type contribution. Perhaps now is the moment to move from a supporting role to a leadership role, or perhaps it is a moment to stand back from the current sphere and move into a new phase of life without the baggage of the previous working environment.

Jean began to recognize that she had held onto some of her attitudes from the commercial world for too long. There was a risk that she kept looking backwards rather than forwards. Jean reached a watershed moment after one year in the charity when she decided that she needed to be more fully committed to the charity. She accepted that she had to live with some of the rough edges and not keep complaining. She told herself that she had to keep believing that she had made the right decision about moving into the charity and see the positive impact that it had on her life. At the same time Jean did not want to lose the commercial edge that came from her previous working life, but she had to apply that commercial edge in a way that was less irritating for her colleagues.

Geoff had been working in supermarkets for a couple of decades. He enjoyed the adrenalin rush when there were problems to address. He liked being around the store on a busy day and feeling the buzz of activity, but how long did he want to stay in this relentless atmosphere? He would dream sometimes of becoming a schoolteacher or setting up his own business or establishing a bed and breakfast property. He recognized that he had particular skills in organizing activity and motivating others; perhaps what he needed was a different store to manage or to move into a different retail space. Various people said to him that he had particular gifts in terms of operational management that were transferable into other sectors. Perhaps he could explore the health world or elsewhere in the distribution industry.

Geoff entered such conversations with bold thoughts about his future but normally at the end of them was happy to revert to being a supermarket manager. He wasn't sure what would both catch his imagination and be an area where he could be successful. The supermarket chain saw him as someone with potential to take on a bigger role. Geoff was unsure whether he would want to go into head office, but his imagination was caught by the opportunity to do an MBA at a local university. Geoff latched onto this as a potential gateway into developing his thinking about what he could do and would want to do beyond managing a supermarket.

Mary had begun to feel worn down by some of the attitudes of Government Ministers she was working with. They seemed more interested in political manoeuvring than delivering successful policy outcomes. She kept getting good feedback on the work she was doing but felt a growing cynicism within her about the political process. Mary did not want to give up the stimulating work she was doing but felt she would benefit from a greater distance from work. In addition she felt exhausted each weekend and thought there must be a way of balancing work and home life more effectively.

Mary had seen a number of examples of job-share arrangements working effectively and decided to explore this as a possible way forward. She much preferred the job-share possibility than working part-time because she wanted to do a mainstream job and not be engaged on some self-contained project. What mattered to her was finding a good colleague who brought a similar set of values and a complementary set of skills. Mary had seen a number of excellent examples of job-share partnerships where individuals were able to combine an interesting role with more time available for family and personal activities and personal renewal. Mary had rejected this option a few years earlier but now recognized that she needed to be bold in making changes to her working life that would enable her to be fresher and a better contributor in the different spheres of life that were important to her.

Bringing an openness to whatever next had become important to Jean, Geoff and Mary. This openness was being expressed in different ways, but in each case it involved being bold and not being caught by previous attitudes or conventions. What was key was a willingness to push the limits of what had previously been their approach and being open to new direction and opportunity.

Questions for reflection

1 How bold or radical are you willing to be in thinking about your next steps?

2 What have you learnt in your current role that will equip you to enter your next phase of life with confidence?

3 What is holding you back from being bold in your decisions going forward?

4 What do you want to characterize your next phase of life?

5 How might hope and opportunity going forward be stronger emotions than reticence or dejection?

About the Author

Peter Shaw has coached individuals, senior teams and groups across six continents. He is a Visiting Professor of Leadership Development at Chester, De Montfort, Huddersfield and Surrey Universities, and is a Professorial Fellow at St John's College, Durham University. He has been a member of the Visiting Professorial Faculty at Regent College, Vancouver, since 2008 and is a Visiting Professor at the Judicial College in Melbourne. He has written 29 books on aspects of leadership, some of which have been translated into seven different languages.

Peter's first career was in the UK Government where he worked in five Government departments and held three Director General posts. He has been a member of governing bodies in higher and further education. He is a licensed lay minister (Reader) in the Anglican Church and plays an active role in the Church of England at parish, diocesan and national levels. He is a Lay Canon of Guildford Cathedral and Chair of Guildford Cathedral Council.

Peter holds a doctorate in Leadership Development from Chester University. He was awarded an honorary doctorate at Durham University for 'outstanding service to public life' and an honorary doctorate by Huddersfield University for his contribution to leadership and management.

In his coaching work Peter enables leaders and teams to use their freedoms as leaders to best effect. Peter draws on his wide experience both as a leader and as a coach to leaders in many different contexts. He seeks to bring insights drawn from his wealth of experience and underpinned by his Christian faith and understanding. His focus is on enabling individuals and teams to increase their effectiveness so that they have a clear vision about what they are seeking to do, apply the values that are most important to them, know how to bring a distinctive value-added approach and recognize their sources of vitality.

Acknowledgements

In the middle of a mentoring conversation with Jim Houston, the then Principal of Regent College, Vancouver, in early 1971, Jim suggested that I might write a book on freedom and responsibility. As I was only 21 I thought this was an idea to park for the long term. As a civil servant for 32 years I wrote a lot in other people's names but never conceived of writing a book. As a coach in my second career I had the opportunity to write in my own name and had logged in the back of my mind that one day I would address the themes of freedom and responsibility.

When visiting Vancouver in 2016 I reminded Jim Houston of what he had said to me 45 years earlier. His comment was, 'Well, it is about time you wrote the book.' As a dutiful former student I thought I ought to rise to that challenge, hence the writing of this book, which is published 50 years after Jim Houston's initial suggestion. I am grateful to Jim for his initial suggestion and his prompting and thoughtfulness.

I am grateful to the many people I have worked with who have been on this journey of learning to use freedom and responsibility wisely. Taking responsibility and sitting lightly to responsibility have been key themes in many coaching conversations. My encouragement in the coaching has been to enable people to see the scope they have to act and use their freedom responsibly. I am indebted to many people for engaging openly with me on these topics and helping me clarify my thinking. Their experience has helped inform the description of the six illustrative and hypothetical characters whose stories are covered in this book.

My thanks go to colleagues at Praesta Partners who have been sources of practical ideas and have always been willing to challenge me. In particular I want to thank Hilary Douglas, Paul Gray, Louise Shepherd and Una O'Brien for their sound perspectives.

I am grateful to Ruth Hannatt and Polly Payne for writing the foreword to this book. Ruth and Polly are the first job-share partnership to hold a Director General post in the UK Government. They are an inspiration to many because of the way they demonstrated what is possible and have not allowed expectations from others to limit their leadership aspiration and impact. They are exemplars in using their freeedoms well in the first leadership roles and cultivating in others a measured and determined sense of responsibility.

Christine Smith at Canterbury Press has been a wise and supportive editor, encouraging me to take forward ideas and turn them into a sequence of books. I am indebted to Rachel Geddes and Hannah Ward for their practical contribution in the editing and proof-reading of the final text.

I am grateful to Zoe Stear who read the manuscript in detail and gave me constructive feedback, encouraging me to set out in more detail my own personal perspective on freedom and responsibility as well as seeking to enable others to use their freedom and responsibilities well. Graham Tomlin's book *Bound to be Free*, published by Bloomsbury, was a helpful prompt with its useful historic background.

I have dedicated my book to Tracy Easthope and Jackie Tookey who have provided wonderful practical support for me in recent years. Tracy has managed my diary with great skill to enable me to have the space to write and to engage with a wide range of different people. Jackie has provided admirable support, typing with great care and efficiency a myriad of different documents as well as the books.

My family have always been supportive of the coaching and writing, and are always ready to tease me when I appear to go into coaching mode. I am indebted to them for their encouragement and to my grandchildren for bringing a sense of fun.

Books and Booklets by Peter Shaw

Mirroring Jesus as Leader (Cambridge: Grove Press, 2004).

Conversation Matters: how to engage effectively with one another (London: Continuum International Publishing, 2005).

The Four Vs of Leadership: vision, values, value-added, and vitality (Chichester: Capstone Press, 2006).

Finding Your Future: the second time around (London: Darton, Longman and Todd, 2006).

Business Coaching: achieving practical results through effective engagement (Chichester: Capstone Press, 2007), co-authored with Robin Linnecar.

Making Difficult Decisions: how to be decisive and get the business done (Chichester: Capstone Press, 2008).

Deciding Well: a Christian perspective on making decisions as a leader (Vancouver: Regent College Publishing, 2009).

Raise Your Game: how to succeed at work (Chichester: Capstone Press, 2009).

Effective Christian Leaders in the Global Workplace (Colorado Springs: Paternoster Press, 2010).

Defining Moments: navigating through business and organisational life (Basingstoke: Palgrave Macmillan, 2010).

The Reflective Leader: standing still to move forward (Norwich: Canterbury Press, 2011), co-authored with Alan Smith.

Thriving in Your Work: how to be motivated and do well in challenging times (London: Marshall Cavendish, 2011).

Getting the Balance Right: leading and managing well (London: Marshall Cavendish, 2013).

Leading in Demanding Times (Cambridge: Grove Press, 2013), co-authored with Graham Shaw.

The Emerging Leader: stepping up in leadership (Norwich: Canterbury Press, 2013), co-authored with Colin Shaw.

100 Great Personal Impact Ideas (London: Marshall Cavendish, 2013).

100 Great Coaching Ideas (London: Marshall Cavendish 2014).

Celebrating Your Senses (Delhi: ISPCK, 2014).

Sustaining Leadership: renewing your strength and sparkle (Norwich: Canterbury Press, 2014).

100 Great Team Effectiveness Ideas (London: Marshall Cavendish, 2015).

Wake Up and Dream: stepping into your future (Norwich: Canterbury Press, 2015).

100 Great Building Success Ideas (London: Marshall Cavendish, 2016).

The Reluctant Leader: coming out of the shadows (Norwich: Canterbury Press, 2016), co-authored with Hilary Douglas.

100 Great Leading Well Ideas (London: Marshall Cavendish, 2016).

Living with Never-ending Expectations (Vancouver: Regent College Publishing, 2017), co-authored with Graham Shaw.

100 Great Handling Rapid Change Ideas (London: Marshall Cavendish, 2018).

The Mindful Leader: embodying Christian principles (Norwich: Canterbury Press, 2018).

100 Great Leading Through Frustration Ideas (London: Marshall Cavendish, 2019).

Forthcoming

The Power of Leadership Metaphors (London: Marshall Cavendish, 2021).

Shaping Your Future (Norwich: Canterbury Press, 2022).

Booklets

Riding the Rapids (London: Praesta, 2008), co-authored with Jane Stephens.

Seizing the Future (London: Praesta, 2010), co-authored with Robin Hindle-Fisher.

Living Leadership: finding equilibrium (London: Praesta, 2011).

The Age of Agility (London: Praesta, 2012), co-authored with Steve Wigzell.

Knowing the Score: what we can learn from music and musicians (London: Praesta, 2016), co-authored with Ken Thompson.

The Resilient Team (London: Praesta, 2017), co-authored with Hilary Douglas.

Job-Sharing: a model for the future workplace (London: Praesta, 2018), co-authored with Hilary Douglas.

The Four Vs of Leadership: vision, values, value-added and vitality (London: Praesta, 2019).

The Resilient Leader (London: Praesta, 2020), co-authored with Hilary Douglas.

Copies of the booklets above can be downloaded from the Praesta website.